"When it comes to achievin[g] ... wisdom is flat wrong. In *Your Best Year Ever*, Michael Hyatt lays out a simple program, backed by the best modern research, to reach your dreams!"

TONY ROBBINS, #1 *New York Times* bestselling author of *Unshakeable*

"Generous goals work (if you write them down), and powerful books work (if you read them). Michael Hyatt has created a fun, fast way to find your dreams and then turn them into reality."

SETH GODIN, author of *Linchpin*

"*Your Best Year Ever* is full of compelling, real-life stories of average people who have achieved extraordinary results. Please take my advice and buy this book only if you want to be able to look back in twelve months and say, 'Now, that was my best year ever!'"

JOHN C. MAXWELL, author, speaker, and leadership expert

"The best part of this book is that before he wrote it, Michael spent decades living it. This is Michael Jordan writing a book about basketball."

JON ACUFF, *New York Times* bestselling author of *Soundtracks* and *All It Takes Is a Goal*

"Let's be honest . . . resolutions just don't work. That's why a lot of gyms are empty and even more budgets are blown by Valentine's Day every year. If you really want things to change over the next twelve months, look at what *Your Best Year Ever* has to say—then do what it says."

DAVE RAMSEY, bestselling author, nationally syndicated radio show host

"Michael has been a trusted friend and guide of mine for a long time. This is a playbook for success in the relationships, endeavors, and beautiful ambitions you have for yourself and the ones you love the most."

BOB GOFF, *New York Times* bestselling author of *Love Does*

"Many people talk about goals, but listen to Michael. He grounds this advice in sound research. A great guide."

DR. HENRY CLOUD, psychologist, *New York Times* bestselling author

"Not only am I having our whole team at FranklinCovey read *Your Best Year Ever*, I am having my three college-age children read it as well. Michael gives us a profound road map for both hope and achievement! This is rare wisdom from an extraordinary leader whom I am grateful to call a friend!"

CHRIS MCCHESNEY, coauthor of *The 4 Disciplines of Execution*

"Throughout your life, you'll meet three types of leaders. The first inspires ambition, without results. The second improves results but ignores the spirit. In *Your Best Year Ever*, Michael Hyatt proves he is the rare third type of leader—one who both raises our performance and lifts our soul."

SALLY HOGSHEAD, *New York Times* bestselling author, creator of How to Fascinate

"Over the last few years, I've referred hundreds of people to Michael Hyatt to help them create their best year ever. Why? His work is based on the best science available, plus the real-world experience of helping more than twenty-five thousand people design their ideal year. I love that he's distilled the best of his work into this book."

JEFF WALKER, #1 *New York Times* bestselling author of *Launch*

"For more than a decade, I've known Michael as a successful leader and entrepreneur. In *Your Best Year Ever*, he shares the simple, proven system he uses to achieve his most important goals. This book can help you achieve even more than you thought possible."

ANDY STANLEY, senior pastor of North Point Community Church, author of *Visioneering*

"Twenty-five thousand students. Twenty years of insight. Fifteen carefully curated chapters. Five unconventional steps. All in one book that will lead you to your best year ever. What could be more essential than that?"

GREG MCKEOWN, *New York Times* bestselling author of *Essentialism*

"Michael Hyatt has written a smart, evidence-based, and often surprising treatise on how to set the right goals and then see them through to completion. A must-read for anyone looking to take systematic steps toward improving their life."

CAL NEWPORT, *New York Times* bestselling author of *Deep Work*

"Michael Hyatt's *Your Best Year Ever* is the best resource on goal setting I've read. It also helps you emphasize your core purpose, which is important because purpose-driven goals are much more likely to be achieved. Get this book. It will show you how to turn your goals into reality."

JON GORDON, *New York Times* bestselling author of *The Energy Bus*

"We all want good things: a rewarding marriage, business, family, spiritual life. Getting them is another story. Thankfully, Michael Hyatt shares what works not only for him but also for the tens of thousands of his Best Year Ever students. I've used this system for years for one simple reason: it's the best available."

DONALD MILLER, *New York Times* bestselling author, founder and CEO of StoryBrand

"Michael Hyatt has a knack for making the complex simple. Even better, he makes it useful. Nothing exemplifies that better than *Your Best Year Ever*. Anyone can put these five steps to work in their own lives today."

DAN SULLIVAN, president of The Strategic Coach Inc.

"I am a Michael Hyatt follower. I have lived out as much of what he teaches as possible. I have paid off all my debt, written books that never would have been published without his inspiration, and taken his advice in many other areas of my life. Now you can do it too. The price of *Your Best Year Ever* is extremely cheap for the *best advice ever*."

STEPHEN ARTERBURN, *New York Times* bestselling author, founder of New Life

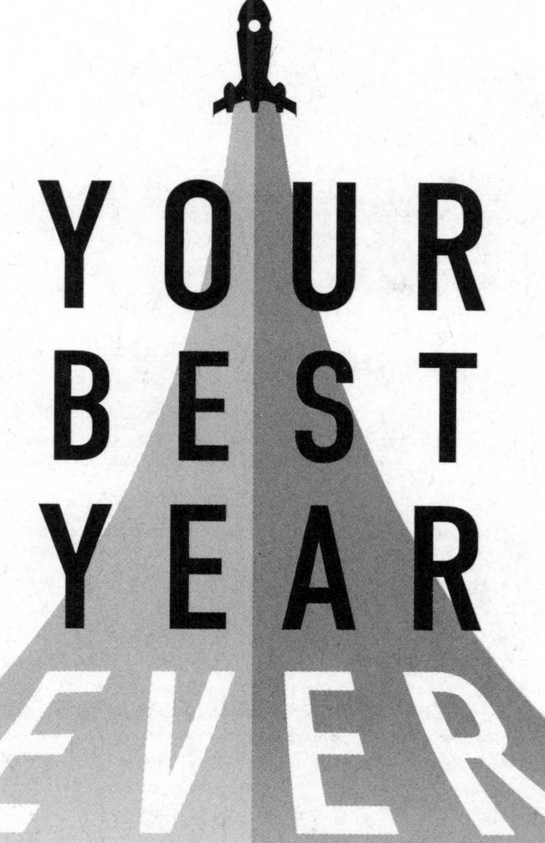

YOUR BEST YEAR EVER

A 5-STEP PLAN FOR ACHIEVING YOUR MOST IMPORTANT GOALS

REVISED AND UPDATED EDITION

MICHAEL HYATT

BakerBooks
a division of Baker Publishing Group
Grand Rapids, Michigan

Published by Baker Books
a division of Baker Publishing Group
Grand Rapids, Michigan
www.bakerbooks.com

Printed in the United States of America

Library of Congress Cataloging-in-Publication Data
Names: Hyatt, Michael, 1955– author.
Title: Your best year ever : a 5-step plan for achieving your most important goals / Michael Hyatt.
Description: Revised and updated edition. | Grand Rapids, Michigan : Baker Books, a division of Baker Publishing Group, [2023] | Includes bibliographical references and index.
Identifiers: LCCN 2023009786 | ISBN 9781540902696 (cloth) | ISBN 9781540903969 (paper) | ISBN 9781493443253 (ebook)
Subjects: LCSH: Intentionalism. | Motivation (Psychology) | Goal (Psychology) | Self-realization.
Classification: LCC BF619.5 .H93 2023 | DDC 153.8—dc23/eng/20230313
LC record available at https://lccn.loc.gov/2023009786

Some names and details of the people and situations described in this book have been changed or presented in composite form in order to ensure the privacy of those with whom the author has worked.

The author is represented by Alive Literary Agency, 7680 Goddard Street, Suite 200, Colorado Springs, CO 80920, www.aliveliterary.com.

Baker Publishing Group publications use paper produced from sustainable forestry practices and post-consumer waste whenever possible.

23 24 25 26 27 28 29 7 6 5 4 3 2 1

Contents

Your Best Is Yet to Come

> Your task is not to foresee the future, but to enable it.
>
> —ANTOINE DE SAINT-EXUPÉRY

> It isn't where you came from; it's where you're going that counts.
>
> —ELLA FITZGERALD

When Edmund Hillary decided he would someday climb Mount Everest, no one really believed he'd do it. Why would they? He was just a beekeeper in New Zealand, a world away. Mountaineering was only a hobby for Hillary. Any talk of climbing the world's tallest, most forbidding mountain sounded crazy. What's more, there had already been several prior attempts on Everest. None had succeeded, and many climbers had died trying. Still, Hillary held on to his dream.

Discharged from the military after an injury in December 1945, Hillary started making that dream a reality. He learned advanced rock and ice climbing and mastered the use of the ice pick, ropes, and other gear required to reach the top, including oxygen equipment for the high altitude. He practiced by climbing peaks in New Zealand and Europe. Finally, in 1951, he got an invitation to the Himalayas on an expedition scouting a path up Everest.

The race was on. Many others in the group were also jockeying for the distinction of being the first to the top. Working with Sherpa guides, the expedition identified the best route up the mountain. They survived avalanches and icefalls, brutal cold, and oxygen deprivation. Then, in 1953, they made another attempt. On May 26, two climbers in the same expedition almost made it to the top, but they failed just a hundred yards from the summit.

Not Hillary. Three days later, on May 29, Edmund Hillary reached the top. He and his Sherpa, Tenzing Norgay, finally crested the 29,000-foot peak. "A few more whacks of the ice-axe, a few very weary steps, and we were on the summit of Everest," Hillary said of the final moments.[1] As far as we know, they were the very first two people in the world to crest the mountain. "We stepped up," Norgay said. "We were there. The dream had come true."[2]

What about you? What's your dream?

Do you have an Everest you want to climb? Is it starting a new business? Getting your health back on track? Doubling your family income? Writing a book? Getting out of debt? Spending more time with family and friends? Mastering a difficult new sport or hobby? Learning a second language so you can experience another part of the world—or more of the one you already inhabit?

Dreams are as diverse as their dreamers. And I believe any dream that inspires you and enhances your life is worth pursuing. You might be pursuing several already. But we all face setbacks. It's part of the pursuit. There's no achievement without some friction, some resistance—maybe lots of it.

Maybe those setbacks lie in your past, informing your present experience. Maybe you're fighting through a major setback right now. If so, you'll identify with Heather Kampf. I think we all can.

Tripped Up by Life

Heather Kampf is a highly decorated runner with an impressive string of accomplishments, including three USA championships for the road mile. But what's most impressive is the time she won first place in the 600-meter final at the 2008 Big Ten Indoor Track Championship after falling flat on her face. For the 600-meter dash, runners make three laps around a 200-meter course. As the third and final lap approached, Kampf was in second place and ready to take first. Then, in a split second, everything changed.

"I was making a move to pass . . . and probably just didn't account for enough space for my long stride," she recalls. "I felt my heel get clipped once, and then on the second time I knew I was going down."[3] More than going down, she went sprawling. Kampf skidded along the ground, her face bouncing on the red track as her momentum tossed her legs up behind her. Spectators gasped. It was a hard fall that instantly knocked her to the rear of the pack with virtually no hope of catching up.

When it comes to achieving our goals, I know a lot of us feel like that. We start out strong and make huge strides, gathering momentum as we go. Then we get derailed or fall short of our hopes. Not always—but often enough that most of us can point to a handful of setbacks or failures with disappointment and regret.

Nothing symbolizes this kind of frustration like New Year's resolutions. People have been making them since forever. Some make them every year, and most of us have made them in the past—six in ten Americans set resolutions at least some years.[4] But just because something is popular doesn't mean it works.

A Faulty System

Hashtags like #resolutionfail start trending on social media hours into the new year. "Got ready for the gym, packed my gear, and went for a burger instead #resolutionfail," a woman joked on January 3. "Bought my twin sister workout clothes for our birthday, and we have yet to lift anything but a fork," another said the next day.[5]

I bet most people can identify. We can usually stick it out a few weeks, but fewer than half are still going after six months. No wonder half of us say resolutions are pointless, and fewer than a quarter of us agree that resolutions have helped improve our lives.[6] The numbers vary depending on the surveys you consult, but ultimate success is elusive to all but a few. In fact, many of us stop making resolutions because we've failed at them in the past.

Welcome to the club. We're like hatchling turtles, bursting with determination to make it over the dunes to the ocean beyond. Then the seagulls swoop in and start picking us off one by one.

Some industries bank on our failure. Fitness centers sell year-long contracts, knowing the majority of customers won't come more than a few weeks. NPR covered a story about one chain with 6,500 members per location but only room for 300 at a time.[7] Gyms can afford to vastly oversell their capacity because they know we'll get distracted or discouraged and lose interest. How does it feel knowing people assume we'll fail—and then benefit when we do?

This is about more than funny tweets and sad statistics. Our goals reflect many of our most important desires and aspirations—our determination to make a change and improve our lives. Consider some common resolutions people set:

- Lose weight and eat healthier
- Be a better person
- Spend less, save more
- Deepen their relationship with God
- Spend more time with family and friends
- Exercise more often
- Learn something new
- Reduce stress
- Do more good deeds for others
- Find the love of their life
- Find a better job[8]

Generally, we're talking about our health, wealth, relationships, and personal development. I get that. My governing assumption in this book is that you're a growth-minded person who wants to excel personally, professionally, relationally, intellectually, and spiritually. And that matters.

When people like you reach their full potential, the world has more happy marriages, kids have their moms and dads at night, businesses have leaders worth admiring and emulating, and you have the health and vitality necessary to fuel your dreams. Through one intentional choice at a time, you make the world around you better. That's exactly why we need a far better plan. Aspirations such as these are too important to entrust to a faulty system.

A Far Better Plan

Some people say the best way to achieve our goals is to play it safe and set only one or two. But for me that's leaving too much on the table—probably for you too. Whether you're an entrepreneur, executive, lawyer, salesperson, designer, marketer, doctor, coach, mom or dad, husband or wife, or several of those things, we're talking about the most important stuff in life. So, why leave so many hopes unfulfilled? Instead of scaling back, we need a system geared to work. We need a proven method to set and achieve our goals.

I've been studying personal development and professional achievement for decades. And I've been practicing both at home and at work. As the former CEO of a $250 million corporation and, today, the founder and chairman of Full Focus, a goal-achievement and coaching company, I utilize a proven system that incorporates safeguards for many of the pitfalls and failings of typical goals and resolutions.

Over the years I've seen amazing results in my own life and in the lives of countless people with whom I've shared the system. I lead thousands through this process every year in our annual Your Best Year Ever Live! event and our Full Focus Goal-Setting course. Not to mention the hundreds of thousands who've learned bits and pieces of the system through our Full Focus podcasts—*The Double Win* and *Focus on This*—and who have put it to use in their own lives with the *Full Focus Planner*™, which has sold more than a million copies as of this writing.

This book emerges from all that learning, living, and teaching. Based on decades of practical experience and the best current research on goal attainment and human achievement, this book is designed to help you find the clarity, develop the courage, and leverage the commitment you need to accomplish your most important personal and professional goals.

Your Breakthrough Year

When Heather Kampf hit the ground, she could have stayed down. She could have easily become discouraged and admitted what everyone was already thinking—that her race was over. "It was as if a vacuum had sucked all the energy out of the place," she says of the moment she collapsed. One of the announcers even tried softening the blow. Since Kampf's teammate had moved into the lead, he said it might be okay if she came in last.

But she didn't.

"The first thing I remember seeing after feeling like I was falling was seeing my hands on the track when I was pushing off to go again," Kampf says. She leapt up as fast as she fell down and began closing the distance. The crowd responded. "As I started to gain momentum, it was like a crescendo of noise and excitement," she remembers.[9] To the amazement of the announcers and spectators, she passed one runner, then another, then finally her own teammate to take *first* place!

Kampf's story provides a powerful picture of what can happen when we stay in the game and keep pushing. Maybe you feel a few steps behind. Maybe you're at the rear of the pack and can't see how you might regain lost ground and reach your goals. Hold that thought.

I want you to consider instead what a true breakthrough year might look like for you. Imagine it's twelve months from now, and you've accomplished your top goals in all of life's domains (more on those in a moment). Think about your health. How does it feel to be in the best shape of your life? How does it feel to have the stamina to play for hours with your kids, pursue your favorite hobbies, and have energy to spare?

Are you married? What's it like to have deepened and enriched your most significant relationship, to feel you can't wait to spend time together? Imagine your life full of intimacy, joy, and friendship with someone who shares your most important priorities, your most significant goals, and who gives the encouragement and support you've dreamt about for so long.

Consider your finances. How does it feel to be debt-free, to have money left over at the end of the month? Imagine having the resources you need to meet your expenses, protect yourself against the unexpected, and invest in the future. Think how reassuring it is to have deep savings and how satisfying it is to provide your family with the life they desire and deserve.

Reflect for a moment on your spiritual life. Imagine you have an abiding sense of something transcendent, of a connection to a larger purpose and a bigger story. Imagine waking up grateful and going to bed satisfied. How does it feel to face life's ups and downs with peace in the deepest part of your soul?

Imagining these possibilities can be difficult for some. Life can feel chaotic and uncertain, and disbelief is one way to brace ourselves for the worst. But I think the reason goes even deeper. Most of us have a long history of not getting what we want out of life. Perhaps we set some big goals we didn't achieve, or the future turned out differently than we planned. Life throws curveballs. We've all been there. Disappointment turns to frustration, to anger, to sadness, and finally twists itself into cynicism. You might feel it rearing its head right now.

I get it—and it's totally normal, even necessary. "The reason we need failure to learn is straightforward," says University of North Carolina professor Bradley Staats. "Learning requires trying new things, and sometimes new things don't work as expected." The good news, he says, is that "failure creates a powerful learning cocktail, mixing new ideas with novel information and a motivation to experiment."[10] But only if you keep an open mind.

Stick with me. Whatever has happened in your past—good or bad—it is truly possible to make this your best year ever, even in those areas where you've suffered serious setbacks. I'm going to show you how. Consider this book an invitation to make the next twelve months the most meaningful and significant you've experienced in your life so far. You might have one or many Everests to climb—and you can reach the top by implementing the system and principles of this book.

What's Your LifeScore?

Your Best Year Ever is based on five key assumptions. First, *real life is multifaceted*. Our lives are more than our work. They are even more than our families. The way I see it, our lives consist of nine interrelated domains:

1. Body: our physical health
2. Mind: our mental health and intellectual engagement
3. Spirit: our connection to God or something greater than ourselves

4. Love: our spouse or significant other
5. Family: our children, parents, and others near and dear to us
6. Community: our friends, associates, and the wider groups we are a part of
7. Money: our personal or family finances
8. Work: our profession or career
9. Hobbies: our pastimes and personal pursuits

Second, *every domain matters*. Why? Because each one affects all the others. For example, your physical condition impacts your work. And stress at work impacts life at home. All this interplay means you've got to give each domain the appropriate attention if you want to experience progress in life.

Third, *progress starts only when you get clear on where you are right now*. Maybe you have a vague sense that things are off track in your career but haven't come to grips with the truth of your situation. Or maybe you sense your marriage has become rote or routine, but you haven't had the courage to just admit you're stuck.

Fourth, *you can improve any life domain*. No matter what's going on in the world or how off track and frustrated you feel, you don't have to settle for what is. Progress and significant personal growth are truly possible. Yes, some things are out of your control. But there's more within your power than you probably realize; it just takes getting started.

And that takes me to the fifth and final assumption: *confidence, happiness, and life satisfaction are byproducts of personal growth*. One of the best ways to overcome all the uncertainty you experience in the world and make progress on your most important goals is to become fully aware of how much

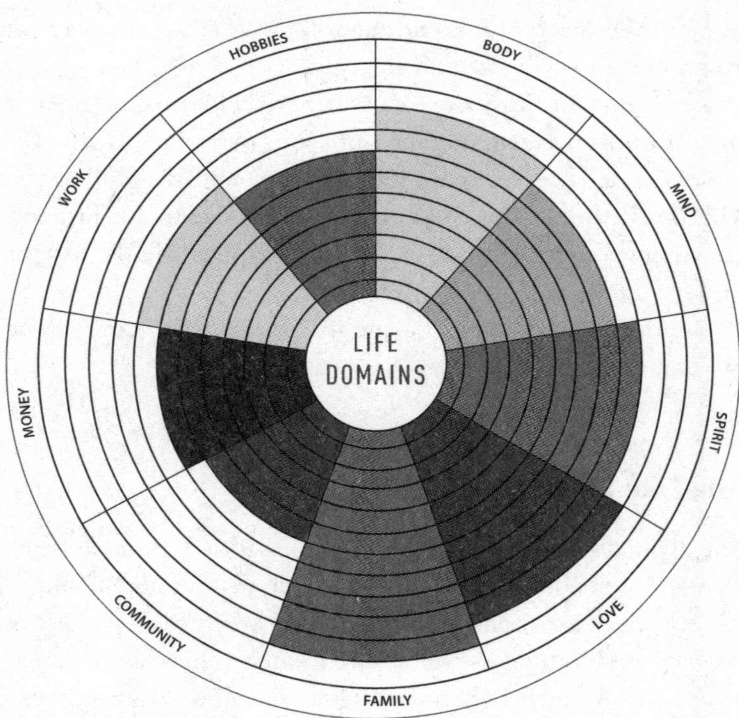

Life consists of nine interrelated domains. Understanding the relative health of each can help you make progress across them all. The example gradations represent relative health in each of the nine life domains for an individual.

agency and control you actually have. It's far more than you think, and it'll grow as you flex it.

To get a sense of where you are right now, I encourage you to take a quick and easy online quiz called the LifeScore® Assessment. You can intentionally engineer massive growth over the next year in the most important domains of life. But you need a baseline on where you are now so you can identify which domains need the most attention. Maybe you're succeeding at work but your health is suffering. Or maybe you're doing a great job connecting at home but don't have an actionable plan to build your savings for an emergency.

I designed the LifeScore Assessment to help you quickly spot areas of improvement and measure your personal growth over time. If you haven't taken it yet, use the QR code or follow the URL at the end of this chapter and get your score. It's fast and easy—just ten minutes. Best of all, it will give you the insight you need to begin your best year ever.

But that's just the start. Let me give you an overview of where we're going next.

The Path Ahead

I've divided my goal-achievement process into five simple steps. In Step 1, I'm going to help you overcome any doubts you might harbor about experiencing your best year ever. Unless we believe we can reach our goals, we're sure to miss. This step will help you shed limiting beliefs and imagine what a breakthrough year might mean for your life.

In Step 2, I'm going to talk to you about getting closure on the past. Dragging the worst of the past into the best of the future is another reason our goals fail. If we get closure on the past, especially those efforts that went unnoticed and unrewarded, we're able to climb our Everests and step into the future. I'm not talking about digging deep into your childhood, just the last few years. I'll give you a four-stage system to analyze what worked and what didn't so you can move forward with the wisdom and insight you need to design the year to come. I'll even show you how some of your biggest frustrations in the last year point to your greatest opportunities in the next.

Then, in Step 3, I'm going to give you a seven-part framework for setting goals that really work. This is where you watch your dreams come to life as you cast your vision for the months ahead. Part of the problem with typical goals and resolutions is that they're poorly designed. Goals like "exercise more often" or "spend less, save more" fail on several counts. Among other things, effective goals are specific and measurable. Goals poorly formulated are goals easily forgotten. This proven framework, on the other hand, will give you a portfolio of meaningful, effective goals.

Another major reason goals fail is that we're not motivated enough to attain them. Without a compelling reason to persist, we lose interest, get distracted, or forget what we purposed to do. In Step 4, I'm going to introduce you to the most powerful motivator I know: your why. Once you nail this piece, you'll be unstoppable, even when the going gets tough and obstacles appear in your path. I'll also show you a foolproof trick for staying motivated while cultivating beneficial new habits.

Finally, in Step 5, we're going to put all the pieces together and empower you to take action with the three best tactics I know for accomplishing the goals you've set. Most goals fail because we're missing proven implementation tactics. Winning a battle takes both strategy and tactics. But unless someone shows us what works best for attaining our goals, we're left to good luck and hard knocks to figure it out on our own. This step will help you flatten the learning curve. This is where you'll learn the power of low-bar next steps, regular goal review, and activation triggers for beating the hurdles that get in the way.

Is this next year just going to be another year, not that different from the rest, or are you going to make this your breakthrough year? You don't have to spend one more year discouraged or disappointed that you're not making the progress you

Goals poorly formulated are goals easily forgotten.

want. If you want to go from frustrated and confused to clear, confident, and empowered, I'm convinced *Your Best Year Ever* has the answers you're looking for.

Let's dive in.

Take Your LifeScore® Assessment
BestYearEver.me/LifeScore

ACTION PLAN

SPARK YOUR ASPIRATIONS

Let's start with one simple step toward your personal Everest right now. Get a notebook, journal, or your *Full Focus Planner*, and jot down a few aspirations. Consider each of the nine domains: body, mind, spirit, love, family, community, money, work, and hobbies. If you've taken the LifeScore Assessment, look at your report. In which domains are you struggling? In which are you thriving?

Let that guide you as you dream and write. To what do you aspire? What mountain(s) will you scale? If you're facing an ambitious Everest like Edmund Hillary was, know that all that matters is placing one foot in front of the other to reach the top. If you've suffered setbacks, be inspired by Heather Kampf. No failures are truly final; they're merely the prelude to what you'll do next.

Start a list of aspirations and keep it with you as you continue reading. Add to it as new ideas come to you.

STEP 1 STEP 2 STEP 3 STEP 4 STEP 5

BELIEVE the POSSIBILITY

There's an old saying: "History doesn't repeat itself, but it rhymes." That's especially true when we're thinking of our personal histories. Why? The circumstances of our lives change week by week, year by year. But we're still us. And our habits of thinking tend to produce consistent results no matter what's going on in our work, our relationships, or the world around us.

If our habits of thinking are beneficial, we tend to experience positive results, such as happiness, personal satisfaction, even material success. If our habits of thinking are counterproductive, on the other hand, we usually experience the opposite: unhappiness, dissatisfaction, and the nagging feeling that the deck is somehow stacked against us, that we're just walking in circles and getting nowhere.

In 2009, researchers from the Max Planck Institute for Biological Cybernetics set out to determine whether humans could walk in a straight line without external cues or pointers. Participants were told to walk for hours in fields, the desert, and forests during various times of day. If they could follow the sun or the moon, people tended to stay on a relatively straight path. But once clouds covered the sky, even if people thought they were going straight, their perception was fallible. Small, random errors veered them off course. Over time, their own paths would cross and loop. The study concludes that people walk in circles due to "increasing uncertainty about where straight ahead is."[1]

Our whole lives, we're asked to walk straight lines without a guide. If you're tired of going in circles, making little progress in life, the good news is that you can change your path. Your aspirations can serve as a compass to keep you moving in the right direction, especially if you take the extra step of turning them into explicit goals, but—and this is the essential point—only if you *believe* those goals can be realized. Beliefs are that powerful, and we'll discover why in the chapters ahead.

Upgrading your beliefs can help, even if your habits of thinking are already serving you well. Whether you're stuck or simply want to level up some area of your life, you can experience transformative personal improvement in all areas of your life by expanding your sense of what's possible. Let's start.

1

Your Beliefs Shape Your Reality

> We live by what we believe, not by what we see.
>
> —ANGELA AHRENDTS

> What happens is of little significance compared with the stories we tell ourselves about what happens.
>
> —RABIH ALAMEDDINE

Several years ago, my wife, Gail, and I had an English setter named Nelson. He was gentle, patient, and great with the grandkids. He had only one fault. Whenever the front door would open, he would bolt like a prison escapee. It could take twenty minutes to chase him down and bring him home. The scariest thing was watching him narrowly escape an oncoming car. We didn't know what to do. Until we discovered Invisible Fence.

It was the breakthrough we needed. It works by pairing an underground perimeter wire to an electronic collar. If Nelson approached the boundary, his collar delivered a warning vibration to stay back. With some additional training, he quickly learned where the line was and avoided it. No more bolting out the door. We could actually leave him in the yard without fear he would run away.

But here's what's interesting. After a while we realized the collar was no longer necessary. If we stood on the other side of the barrier and called, he wouldn't come. If the kids tried to entice him with a treat, he wouldn't budge. The barrier had moved from the external world of an electronic device to the internal world of Nelson's head.

The Power of Beliefs

Our beliefs play a massive part in how we approach life. Why? We tend to experience what we expect. And we've known this for a long time.

"If men define situations as real, they are real in their consequences," sociologist William I. Thomas said in 1928. Reflecting on "the Thomas theorem" twenty years later, sociologist Robert K. Merton coined the phrase "self-fulfilling prophecy." In 1957, philosopher Karl Popper labeled it the "Oedipus effect," after the mythic hero whose life fulfilled a tragic prophecy. More recently, science writer David Robson has described what he calls the "expectation effect," diving deep into the impact of mindset and perspective on the results we experience.[1]

As Chris Berdik, another science writer, says in his book *Mind Over Mind*, "Our real world is in many ways an expected world. What we see, hear, taste, feel, and experience is produced from the top down as much as it is from the bottom up. Our minds organize chaos. We fill in blanks with well-learned forms, patterns, and assumptions. Our predictions for the near and distant future bend reality."[2] How?

It's not fantasy. Nor is it related to any supposed law of attraction, as some might think. It's actually far simpler than that. Because our expectations shape what we believe is possible, they shape our perceptions and actions. That means they also shape the outcomes. And that means they shape our reality.

Remember the old Tiger Woods? The pre-meltdown Woods who burnt up the record books year after year? Some of his clutch shots are legendary. At the 2003 Presidents Cup in South Africa, for example, he sunk a fifteen-foot putt in the near dark. It seemed like an impossible shot. Everyone thought so—but not Woods. Listen to what his teammate Mike Weir has said about that shot: "He knew he was going to make it. . . . That's probably what separated him more than anything else: his belief."[3] Do you hear what Weir is saying? Many other golfers had the skill to make those shots, but they lacked the belief they could pull it off.

That's true for a lot of us.

Our expectations come from our mindset. According to Stanford University psychologist Carol Dweck, there are two primary orientations: the fixed mindset and the growth mindset.[4] We can have a mix of both, depending on our circumstances.

It's probably safe to say that neither is inherently good or bad, but a growth mindset has been shown to better serve goal achievement. Building on this idea, psychologist Kelly McGonigal says that "changing our minds can be a catalyst for all the other changes we want to make in our lives," but the trick is that we first "need to convince ourselves that such change is possible."[5] We need to believe that we can pull it off.

The Problem with Doubts

What's one of the biggest reasons we don't succeed with our goals? We simply doubt we can. We believe they're out of reach.

When pollsters asked respondents to an *Economist*/YouGov survey how confident they were about sticking to their New

Year's resolutions, only 37 percent said "very confident." Six in ten were only somewhat confident, not very confident, or not at all confident.[6] Is it any wonder we struggle to make progress?

Polls show the percentage of people in their twenties who achieve their New Year's resolutions is far greater than those over fifty. In fact, while eight in ten millennials set resolutions, almost seven in ten adults over sixty-five say setting resolutions is "a waste of time," according to a Harris Poll.[7] Why? It's sad, but the greater the number of setbacks we've experienced in life, the less likely we are to believe we can prevail. Doubt is a goal toxin.

To shield ourselves from future disappointment, we develop a cynical, self-protective attitude toward life. We're like my dog Nelson. We've tried to step out in the past and have been zapped—or far worse. Maybe it was only once. Or maybe it was several times. Regardless, now we stand still even when there is no actual barrier. The one in our heads is strong enough to keep us stuck.

You know what this looks like:

- You say, "I need to apply for that new job." But then you think, *There's no way. I don't have enough experience or enough education.*
- A friend says, "Hey, you and Bill should go to that marriage retreat this weekend." And you think, *Are you kidding me? I can't get him off the couch for an evening, let alone a whole weekend.*
- Somebody says, "I think it would be awesome to run a 5K." And you think, *Maybe I should*. But then the cynicism sets in. *I'm 40 pounds overweight*, you think. *I've got a bum knee. There's no way I could possibly run a 5K.*

One thing these three examples have in common: doubt. Another thing: subsequent inaction. Take any idea that might take you to the next chapter of your story, apply some doubt, and the whole thing just withers and dies.

Some doubt comes from self-protection. It's hard to get your hopes dashed if you never get them up to begin with. You can see this sort of thing in the numbers. When asked how they think a new year would compare with the prior one, only 38 percent of poll respondents said they think their life would improve. Sixty-two percent said their life would either stay the same or even get worse. Think about that: the majority of the population expects either stasis or decline![8]

That kind of attitude poisons our souls and sabotages our results. Our beliefs about what's possible have a direct impact on our behavior in the present and the reality we experience in the future. But what if you could change your sense of what's possible?

A Different Frame

Triple-A baseball pitcher Steve Mura was starting one night in an away game, but he almost lost before leaving the dugout. Why? "I can never win on this mound," he told his pitching coach, Harvey Dorfman. Dorfman didn't buy that for a second. But he could see Mura was already preparing to lose. So Dorfman pushed Mura to explain his belief. The pitcher said the angle of the mound was wrong. And for Mura, that settled it. But not for his coach. It was just a jumping-off point.

Dorfman asked what kind of adjustments he could make. Sounds simple, I know. But it was like a switch. That one suggestion created a new sense of possibility. Before the game, Mura

What if you could change your sense of what's possible?

came up with a new strategy to deal with the unfriendly slope of the mound. "There is a difference," Dorfman told Mura, "between, 'I have not won' and 'I cannot win.'" The past didn't determine the future—unless Mura's belief led him to act like it did. "You don't think about strategies when you think that outcome is inevitable," Dorfman said. But by changing his belief, Mura was able to change his strategy and the outcome. He pitched an almost-perfect game that night—just two hits and no runs.[9]

Mura faced a major challenge. But like Nelson, it was in his mind, not on the field. I find that's true for almost all areas of life. "Many of the circumstances that seem to block us in our daily lives may only appear to do so based on a framework of assumptions we carry with us," say Rosamund Stone Zander and Benjamin Zander. "Draw a different frame around the same set of circumstances and new pathways come into view."[10] Changing your thinking is like flipping a switch; it creates a new sense of possibility, along with different results.

There's a popular story about a shoemaker who sent two salesmen to Africa to size up the market. The first reported back, "No one here wears shoes. There's no market." But the second said, "No one here wears shoes. Huge opportunity! Send inventory!" Facts are facts. But we can look at them in different ways.

I'm about 99.9 percent certain that story is made up, but there's a real version of the tale that demonstrates the same point. In 1999, Nick Swinmurn thought he could sell shoes online. But investors thought it would never fly: too many logistical and customer-service challenges. And the opportunity seemed minuscule; at the time, the nearest comparison was mail-order shoe sales, which was a measly 5 percent of the market. Not surprisingly, most investors wouldn't return his calls.

One investor, however, heard something in Swinmurn's pitch that made his ears perk. The mail-order business was only 5 percent of the market, but that market was $40 billion! If catalog sales were already $2 billion, the logistical and customer-service challenges must not have been that big a deal. The market was potentially massive. And just like that, Zappos was born. Amazon purchased the company a decade later for $1.2 billion.[11] Investors all heard the same original pitch. Only one brought a different sense of possibility to the facts.

History is full of similar stories. What's amazing is that once people realize something is possible, others quickly come behind and duplicate or even best the feat. We started the book with Edmund Hillary and Tenzing Norgay's achievement at Everest; as of this writing, more than six thousand others have also now done the once impossible and summited Everest.[12]

Pilots once thought it was impossible to fly faster than 768 miles an hour (the speed of sound at sea level). But Chuck Yeager figured he could do it and officially broke the sound barrier on October 14, 1947. Planes have only advanced since then, and pilots regularly fly two, four, even six times the speed of sound.

Before 1954, runners assumed it was impossible to run a mile in less than four minutes. Then Roger Bannister ran it in three minutes, fifty-nine seconds, and change—a record that has since been beaten by other runners.

For a long time, the idea of running a marathon in under two hours seemed impossible. But in 2019, Kenyan runner Eliud Kipchoge shocked the world by breaking the two-hour barrier at an unsanctioned exhibition marathon. He finished in one hour, fifty-nine minutes, and forty seconds. That doesn't count for the record, but it's ridiculously fast regardless.

When it comes to sanctioned races, Kipchoge is faster than anyone else in the world. In September 2022, Kipchoge ran the Berlin Marathon in two hours, one minute, and nine seconds.[13] The distance between Kipchoge's official record and his doing the supposedly impossible is about half the time it should take you to brush your teeth each morning.

What's his secret? He credits his thinking. As he told one reporter in 2017, "The difference only is thinking. . . . You think it's impossible, I think it's possible."[14] He told *Runner's World*, "Personally, I don't believe in limits."[15] Nor does he stop; Kipchoge uses his mindset to continually outdo his own performances.[16] Kipchoge's outlook empowers him to achieve the extraordinary, and the same outlook has empowered countless others to attain the impossible in their lives too.

Here's another example. People have dreamt about human-powered flight for millennia, but it always seemed like the stuff of fantasy. Then, in 1977, someone developed an engineless plane capable of sustained, controlled flight. That was just the start. In 1988, Greek cycling champion Kanellos Kanellopoulos flew more than seventy miles over open sea all by pedal power.[17] And he's not the only one; building and flying people-powered aircraft is a weekend hobby for some nowadays.

In the mid-1980s, skateboarder Mike McGill did the first ever 540-degree aerial turn in his sport. That's a full rotation and a half. No one thought it could be done, but once McGill finally did the "McTwist," others began doing it too, pushing it further still. Tony Hawk did the first-ever 720-degree turn, then a 900. And then, in 2012, Tom Schaar—at just twelve years old—did the first-ever 1080. That's three full rotations in the air! As Schaar told ESPN, "It was the hardest trick I've ever done, but"—and get this—"it was easier than I thought."[18] Amazingly, in 2019, Mitchie Brusco bested that record, doing the first 1260![19]

It's true that beliefs are not enough on their own. Skills are required, of course. Writing about athletes pursuing the heights of personal performance, Alex Hutchinson puts it this way: "Training is the cake and belief is the icing—but sometimes the thin smear of frosting makes all the difference."[20] Pair equally matched athletes in a competition; the one with the edge is the one with the better head game.

The impossible only seems so on the front end. Yeager, Bannister, Kanellopoulos, McGill, Hawk, and Schaar—they showed the rest of us that more was attainable than we previously believed. "The greatest developments in history are the result of someone wanting something that did not yet exist," says Luke Burgis, "and helping others to want more than they thought wantable."[21] That can be you.

"Whatever you think can't be done, somebody will come along and do it," said jazz pianist Thelonious Monk.[22] Will you be the next Kipchoge or Brusco and take it even further? Will you inspire others to do the same?

A Failure of Imagination

The first key difference between an unmet goal and personal success is the belief that it can be achieved. Listen to what famed futurist, sci-fi author, and inventor Arthur C. Clarke says: "When a distinguished but elderly scientist states that something is possible, he is almost certainly right. When he states that something is impossible, he is very probably wrong." As Clarke says, it's a "failure of imagination."[23]

And it's not just scientists. That failure of imagination affects athletes, parents, leaders, managers, teachers, and the rest of us to one degree or another. We need to start with shifting our mindsets. Broadly speaking, there are two ways to look at life. One leads directly to the failure of imagination. But the other can revive and amplify our sense of possibility. We'll look at the difference next.

2

Some Beliefs Hold You Back

How little we see! What we do see depends mainly on what we look for.

—JOHN LUBBOCK

Life is change. Growth is optional. Choose wisely.

—KAREN KAISER

I once had a client whom I'll call Charlie. That's not his real name. Let's just say I've changed his identity to protect the guilty. Charlie derived significance from feeling wronged, put upon, and persecuted. He griped about everything. Everyone was an idiot but him. Nobody could do anything right. Life was rigged. If we went to lunch, which I dreaded, he never picked up the check—even if he called the meeting. I always left his presence drained and diminished.

And it wasn't just me. Charlie was that way with everyone. His employees and friends rolled their eyes when I mentioned his name. He approached every relationship with a hoarding mentality. People around him lived in constant fear that their livelihood and well-being were at risk. And guess what? The success he craved always seemed out of reach.

Charlie exemplifies what I call *scarcity thinking*.

Now, compare Charlie with another friend of mine. Amy is one of the most generous people I know. She always greets me with an enthusiastic smile, a big hug, and an encouraging word. I always leave her presence energized, feeling great about being me. And she's like this with everyone. She treats friends, employees, clients, vendors, and everyone else, even business competitors, with generosity and grace. She routinely invests in their success, and it comes back to her in a thousand ways. Amy exemplifies what I call *abundance thinking*.

Scarcity vs. Abundance

To accomplish anything, we have to believe we're up to the challenge. That doesn't mean it will be easy or that we even know how we're going to accomplish it—usually we don't know. It just means we believe we're capable; we believe we have what it takes to prevail.

Why is that important? Because every goal has obstacles. When some people have trouble getting over those obstacles, they doubt they have what it takes. Think Charlie. But others are confident they'll prevail if they just work harder or come at the problem from a different direction. Think Amy.

Researchers label the first group *entity theorists*, or people with *fixed* mindsets. They think their abilities are set in stone. You've heard people say this: "I'm just no good at *x*, *y*, or *z*." These are the scarcity thinkers. They assume if something doesn't come easily, it's probably not for them. Scarcity thinking naturally leads to limiting beliefs. Assessments reveal that about four in ten students and adults possess this mindset.

Researchers call the second group *incremental theorists*, or those with *growth* mindsets. When they struggle with an obstacle, they just look for new approaches to the problem. They know there's a workaround or a solution if they just keep working at it. If something is tantalizingly out of reach, it must be worth the trouble of going for it; they'll figure out how to make it happen as they try. These are the abundance thinkers, and their mindset naturally leads not to limiting beliefs but to liberating truths. Research shows there are about as many people out there with this mindset as there are with the other. Two in ten sit on the fence.[1]

Of these two habits of thinking, one leads to failure, fear, and discontent. The other leads to success, joy, and fulfillment.

SCARCITY THINKERS	**ABUNDANCE THINKERS**
1. Are entitled and fearful	1. Are thankful and confident
2. Believe there will never be enough	2. Believe there is always more where that came from
3. Are stingy with their knowledge, contacts, and compassion	3. Are happy to share their knowledge, contacts, and compassion with others
4. Assume they are the way they are	4. Assume they can learn, grow, and develop
5. Default to suspicion and aloofness	5. Default to trust and openness
6. Resent competition, believing it makes the pie smaller and them weaker	6. Welcome competition, believing it makes the pie bigger and them better
7. Are pessimistic about the future, believing that tough times are ahead	7. Are optimistic about the future, believing the best is yet to come
8. See challenges as obstacles	8. See challenges as opportunities
9. Think small and avoid risk	9. Think big and embrace risk
10. Want to guard their piece of the pie	10. Want to bake bigger pies

The main difference? Scarcity thinkers like Charlie operate from a web of limiting beliefs about the world, other people, and themselves, whereas abundance thinkers like Amy operate from a foundation of liberating truths.

The big question now is this: What's your mindset? Achieving our goals starts by understanding the distinction between these two mindsets and the beliefs that characterize them. Scarcity thinking is marked by limiting beliefs, while abundance thinking fuels liberating truths.

Don't be surprised if you've got a bit of both Charlie and Amy in you; we all do. In fact, it can change with the situation we find ourselves in. Someone may show signs of scarcity thinking in one area of their life and abundance in another.[2] The trick is recognizing scarcity thinking when it crops up.

3 Kinds of Limiting Beliefs

It's easy to spot limiting beliefs in our own thinking if we're attentive. Start with assumptions we hold about the world. "I can't start a new business right now; the market is terrible," somebody might say. Or, "I don't trust management; they're always trying to cheat us." Or, "Those politicians are going to deep-six the economy and make it impossible for me to get ahead."

These can be very deep-seated beliefs. But they're not always reality, and they're rarely the whole truth, even when they seem accurate. We've got to learn to question and even dismiss them or they will limit our freedom and motivation to act.

We also have limiting beliefs about others. "It's no use asking," you might say. "He's too busy to meet with me." Or, "Hey, she's just a bean counter. What can she possibly know?" Or,

3 KINDS OF LIMITING BELIEFS

ABOUT THE WORLD

ABOUT OTHERS

ABOUT OURSELVES

Watch out: limiting beliefs distort our view of the world, others, even ourselves.

"He hasn't responded yet. I guess he must be upset with me." Or, "Someone like her would never go out with a person like me." These aren't truths necessarily. They're just beliefs we let influence us.

The third type of limiting belief is what really hits home for most of us. I mean beliefs about ourselves. We might say, "I'm a quitter. I never finish what I start." Or, "I can't help it. I've never been physically fit." Or, "I've always been terrible with money." Or, "I'm just not the creative type." These beliefs are often false, half-truths at best. And they will roadblock any progress you want to make in life.

How do you know if you're falling into the trap of limiting beliefs? In his book *Making Habits, Breaking Habits*, Jeremy Dean mentions three dead giveaways:

- *Black-and-white thinking.* That's when we assume we've failed if we don't achieve perfection. Reality is usually a sliding scale, not a toggle switch.
- *Personalizing.* That's when we blame ourselves for random negative occurrences.
- *Catastrophizing.* That's when we assume the worst, even with little evidence.[3]

To that list we can add a fourth:

- *Universalizing.* That's when we take a bad experience and assume it's true across the board.

Our language offers a dead giveaway for limiting beliefs. If our words betray "either/or" appraisals of the world, others, or ourselves, we're in trouble—same if we catch ourselves self-bullying or doom-spiraling over an unpleasant or unwanted occurrence. And, as my daughter Megan reminds me, if you use broad-brush words like *never*, *always*, *can't*, *won't*—anything a marriage therapist says you should avoid in communication with your spouse—your vocabulary is throwing up flags about your mindset: you're in limiting beliefs land. The key is to put a speed bump between your experiences and the stories you're telling yourself about those experiences.[4]

So, where do these beliefs come from?

The Source of Limiting Beliefs

Some of our limiting beliefs, as I've said, come from previous failures or setbacks. Repeated setbacks can train us to assume the worst. They can condition us to hoard what we have and avoid risks.

But if we're observant, we can spot other influences. The news media, for instance, has a strong negativity bias. As J. R. R. Tolkien quipped, it's mostly murders and football scores.[5] "Studies have shown that an overabundance of news can make you depressed, anxious, and, for the most part, doesn't usually provide you with the ability to actually change or influence anything being reported," says Michael Grothaus—and he's a professional journalist.[6]

Reality is usually a sliding scale, not a toggle switch.

Tune in, and it's easy to believe the world is getting worse and worse—more crime, more poverty, more violence than ever. It's like a long litany of worry and fear, interrupted by commercials about scary medical conditions. News organizations are predisposed to show you negative news because fear triggers the more primitive parts of our brains and keeps our eyes glued to the threat. To make matters worse, their industry is in decline. So the media increasingly appeal to fear in order to deliver eyeballs to their advertisers.

Then there's social media, which can mirror this negativity bias. After an election cycle, it can seem like a never-ending stream of negativity. But you can also detect a positivity bias at work.

Check Instagram, and it can seem like everyone's leading a charmed life. Happy kids, beautiful friends, gorgeous vacations, fulfilling work. We're instantly, usually subconsciously, aware we're not measuring up. We're not as smart, creative, educated, successful, lucky, athletic, or artistic as everyone else.

Scholar Donna Freitas conducted a large-scale study of social media and students on more than a dozen college campuses. "Facebook is the CNN of envy, a kind of 24/7 news cycle of who's cool, who's not, who's up, and who's down," she writes in *The Happiness Effect*, a book that reports her findings. "Unless you have rock-solid self-esteem, are impervious to jealousy, or have an extraordinarily rational capacity to remind yourself exactly what everyone is doing when they post their glories on social media [that is, positioning and bragging], it's difficult not to care."[7] I'm a huge advocate of social media, but it's no wonder that time on Facebook is predictive of feeling crummy about our lives.[8]

And then there are negative relationships, anyone from friends and coworkers to our family or faith community. We often pick up limiting beliefs from other people in childhood.

These beliefs become part of what University of Virginia psychology professor Timothy Wilson calls our "core narratives" about life.[9] Many of these core narratives are good and helpful. But some are not, and they can be hard to let go of and disruptive when we try. Other times we pick up limiting beliefs later in life at church, the college quad, or the office. Regardless of when or where we acquire them, our beliefs create the lens through which we see the world.

"The undeniable reality is that how well you do in life and business depends not only on what you do and how you do it . . . but also on who is doing it with you or to you," psychologist Henry Cloud says in *The Power of the Other*.[10] Hang around people like Charlie, and you start seeing the world from his glum, self-defeating perspective. Surround yourself with Amys, on the other hand, and everything starts looking up.

It's worth noting that these mindsets become self-reinforcing. Cognitive neuroscientist and journalist Christian Jarrett describes a dynamic we can see operating in our lives if we're observant. Our personalities, he says, are a mix of nature and nurture. Our genes and biology combine with our life experiences to form our personalities, which include our beliefs about the world, others, and ourselves. Our personalities then drive how we act and react in the world while we pursue what we want.

What's striking about Jarrett's model is the loop. As our actions and reactions shape our experience of the world, that experience feeds back into our personality. It's a self-reinforcing circle: our beliefs shape our experience, and our experience shapes our beliefs, creating a virtuous or vicious cycle, depending on what beliefs we embrace and enact.[11]

The thing to realize is that positivity and negativity are, to one degree or another, both learned and changeable. They're perspectives, not facts. And remember when I said we've all got some Charlie and Amy in us? That's important to recognize so that we can intentionally shift our mindset to something more empowering when we notice disempowering beliefs creeping in—because we inevitably will from time to time.

If we want to experience our best year ever, we have to begin by recognizing which of these two kinds of thinking dominates and intentionally move toward abundance. There's no reason to let limiting beliefs hold us back.

You Choose

Shortly after Apple CEO Steve Jobs died in 2011, family, friends, and others gathered at Memorial Church on the Stanford University campus. The invitation-only event drew several hundred to pay tribute to a visionary innovator and leader they had come to admire, respect, and love. Journalist Brent Schlender recounts the moment at the close of his book *Becoming Steve Jobs*.

Bono, Joan Baez, and Yo-Yo Ma performed. Oracle founder Larry Ellison spoke, as did lead Apple designer Jony Ive. But what struck Schlender the most were the words of Jobs's wife, Laurene Powell. "He shaped how I came to view the world," she said of her husband, adding,

> It is hard enough to see what is already there, to remove the many impediments to a clear view of reality, but Steve's gift was even greater: he saw clearly what was not there, what could be there, what had to be there. His mind was never a captive of reality. Quite the contrary. He imagined what reality lacked, and he set out to remedy it.

As a result, she said, Jobs possessed "an epic sense of possibility."[12]

So, ask yourself: What's not in your world right now that could be, must be there? What's lacking that only you can remedy in your relationships, your health, your career, or your spiritual life? As we begin to think about designing our best year ever, we need to recognize that most of the barriers we face are imaginary.

Sometimes those barriers feel fixed; they feel certain. Mount Everest is 29,000 feet high. Mountaineers had made many attempts on its summit, but they couldn't seem to get past the final 1,000 feet of elevation. Some died trying. "It almost seemed as though there was some invisible barrier at 28,000 feet through which no man could go," Edmund Hillary said.[13] Imagine if he and everyone else looked at the results up to that point and decided it was truly impossible.

There are a million thoughts running through our heads, but we alone get to choose what we're going to believe. And the best way to overcome limiting beliefs is to replace them with liberating truths. It's possible to upgrade our beliefs. More on that next.

3

You Can Upgrade Your Beliefs

Impossible is not a fact. It's an opinion.

—AIMEE LEHTO

Is not everything impossible until it is done?

—DANIEL WILSON

In 1954, Martin Luther King Jr. accepted the ministerial call from Dexter Avenue Baptist Church in Montgomery, Alabama. He was just twenty-five years old. But what King accomplished over the next decade would radically reshape American society.

In 1955, after Rosa Parks famously refused to give up her seat, King led the Montgomery bus boycott. The US Supreme Court sided with the boycotters in 1956. A year later, King formed and led the Southern Christian Leaders Conference, which helped organize the burgeoning civil rights movement. He also spoke before his first national audience and made the cover of *Time* magazine. But that was only the beginning.

King's organizing and protest work continued in the late fifties and early sixties with sit-ins and protests, culminating in the events of 1963. That April, King was arrested in Birmingham for disobeying a ban on demonstrations. When he came under fire from local ministers, he responded with one of his most important and memorable works, "Letter from a Birmingham Jail." A few months later, he led the March on Washington, attended by over two hundred thousand people.

It was the hundredth anniversary of Lincoln's Emancipation Proclamation, and King gave his stirring "I Have a Dream" speech from the steps of the Lincoln Memorial. The demonstration galvanized nationwide support for civil rights. Earlier that summer, President John F. Kennedy had introduced the nation's most sweeping civil rights legislation to date, and the impact of the march and King's advocacy was instrumental in its passage in 1964.

If that weren't enough, *Time* picked King as its person of the year, and the Nobel committee made him the youngest-ever recipient of the Peace Prize. There was more work to do, but he'd already turned the world upside down. He was just thirty-five years old. What was his secret?

Avoiding the Trap of Limiting Beliefs

King's critics in Birmingham considered his actions "unwise and untimely."[1] But unlike King, these ministers were laboring under a limiting belief: they held an idea about the world that limited their range of possibilities. Instead of seeing King's actions as paving the way for change, they saw them as counterproductive. They worried his actions would cause them to lose ground. But this is just one of a million examples in life where "received wisdom" is simply another way of saying "widely held misunderstanding."

As we learned in the last chapter, a limiting belief is a misunderstanding of the present that shortchanges our future. King was surrounded by limiting beliefs such as these:

- The civil rights movement is asking for too much too fast.
- The movement is stirring up unnecessary trouble.
- Nonviolence won't move the needle. Armed resistance is needed.
- White people won't change. Racial reconciliation is impossible.
- Racism is ingrained in the culture. We'll never change that, let alone the law.

And there were many, many others shared by both White and Black people, inside and outside the movement. The difference between King and others was that he rejected those beliefs as untrue. Instead, he believed that the times called for urgent action. He believed that nonviolent demonstrations were necessary and effective. He believed that racial reconciliation

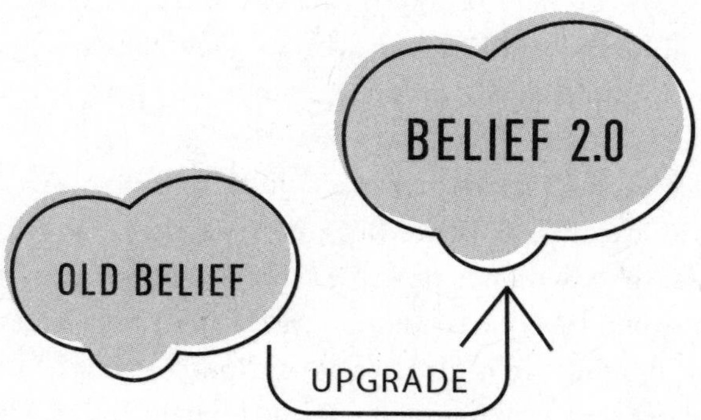

Beliefs can keep us stuck. But we can get unstuck by upgrading our beliefs.

was a real hope and that hearts—and the whole of society—could really change.

Instead of limiting beliefs, King embraced liberating truths. He looked at the same facts as everyone else, but he used a different frame, to use the Zanders' language from earlier. That's what his "I Have a Dream" speech was all about.

King could see a better future, regardless of what some people said or believed. His frame allowed him to visualize the victory, and he knew in his bones that he would someday realize it as well. These liberating truths freed him to act with determination—and we can do the same thing.

Trade Your Frame

Few of our aspirations will measure up to the accomplishments of Martin Luther King Jr. But they do matter to the one and only life we'll ever have. And they can make all the difference in the world for us and the people nearest to us.

One of my favorite examples of replacing limiting beliefs with liberating truths comes from the Alcoholics Anonymous community. Researchers at Brown University, UC Berkeley, and the National Institutes of Health worked together on a major study. They found that the difference maker for people trying to stay sober is belief.

Instead of saying, "I can't resist a drink," people in AA find they actually can resist. Why? Because now they believe the liberating truth "Change is possible." Or instead of thinking, "I can't get sober," AA participants swap that for the liberating truth "I can manage life's difficulties without a drink."[2]

Here's another example from my friend Donald Miller. Don's a bestselling author and tremendous entrepreneur. But after a string of failed relationships, he figured he was doomed at love. Then out of the blue, Bob Goff called.

"You know what I've noticed about you, Don?" Bob started. "I've noticed that you're good at relationships." Don wasn't buying. He was terrible at relationships, and he knew it for certain. But Bob kept calling him and telling him the opposite.

He gave example after example of times Don had really bonded with people. "For the next few months there was a yawning chasm between Bob's affirmation and the way I felt about myself," Don said. But Bob's persistence paid off. "Like a trial lawyer, he argued his case into my soul, week after week, until the chasm began to close."

Don realized Bob was right. And the more he realized it, the more he was able to act on it and prove it to himself. The new belief enabled him to be vulnerable, hopeful, and act with confidence. It turned out Don was terrific at relationships—and he went on to date and marry the love of his life.[3]

Let me give you some examples from my own life. I used to believe I wasn't good with my hands. I was always intimidated by anything mechanical. As soon as I could afford it, I would just hire other people to do that kind of work for me. I didn't enjoy those tasks—or so I thought. But in recent years I started noticing that I enjoy washing the dishes; it may sound like an odd thing to say, but I'm really good at it. And it gives me a sense of accomplishment and contribution. I filed this away in my brain.

Then I decided to try my hand at installing an automated lighting system. I have zero electrical experience, but I thought to myself, *I'll bet I can learn how to do this simply by watching YouTube videos.* Sure enough, I was right. I installed the entire system. I loved learning something new, and it gave me enormous satisfaction to do the project. I'm still enjoying the system to this day. Since that time, I've installed a live-streaming studio in my office, which involved some fairly complicated wiring and setup.

How did things turn around so completely? When I recognized that thought about not being good with my hands as a limiting belief, I replaced it with a liberating truth. Less Charlie, more Amy. I started saying, "I'm very good with my hands. I can learn anything." It didn't feel that way at first. But instead of operating from scarcity, I chose to operate from a place of abundance. And now I'm much more confident whenever a new project comes along.

I've wrestled with limiting beliefs around money in the past as well. I nearly went bankrupt in 1992. My business failed, and people from church had to bring my family groceries for us to make it. Along with that, a mentor once told me, "You're not very good with money, are you?" I took those two experiences and created a story: "I'm not very good with money." It took me years to shake myself loose of that, but I did. I started noticing when I handled money well. I also noticed the frequency—most of the time. I intentionally started telling myself that I was good with money and I could get even better.

Similarly, I used to believe I couldn't get ahead because I could barely make enough money to meet our family's needs. When I recognized that thought as a limiting belief, I determined to replace it with a liberating truth. So I started saying, "I have all the money I need to meet our obligations, accomplish our goals, and be generous with others." It sure didn't feel that way at first. But instead of operating from scarcity, I chose to operate from a place of abundance. It wasn't magic. But it did open new pathways that allowed me to move forward. And the more I moved, the more resources I found to improve my circumstances.

Here's another: "I don't feel like doing that right now," I used to say. "I'm exhausted." I thought my energy was something I had no control over. Either I felt energetic or not. But then I realized I had agency. I could influence what I experienced. So I swapped that limiting belief for a liberating truth that went like this: "I have more than enough energy to accomplish the tasks I undertake." I repeated that to myself every time I felt exhausted or tired. It wasn't long before my reality caught up to my words. In all these examples, changing beliefs made better outcomes possible. It's not magic. You already have what it takes to move the needle in your life.

Everyone's different, and we all have our own portfolio of limiting beliefs. But in all my coaching, I've encountered two that many of us share. The first is that we have no power to change our circumstances, and the second is that we lack the resources to do so. I want to look at both of these in turn.

When We Feel Powerless

Erin Gruwell was a rookie schoolteacher assigned to a tough, newly integrated high school in Long Beach, California. Her diverse classroom was packed with at-risk kids, some of them rival gang members who hated their teacher even more than they hated each other.

"My class has become a dumping ground for disciplinary transfers, kids in rehab or those on probation," Gruwell said.[4] Most everyone had given up on these students. The administration didn't hold much hope that she could make a difference. Even her dad thought she should find a new job. Fortunately for her students, Gruwell believed she could succeed with these kids where others had failed.

She started by chucking the standard curriculum and assigning books about teens dealing with crises, including Anne Frank's *The Diary of a Young Girl* and Zlata Filipović's *Zlata's Diary: A Child's Life in Wartime Sarajevo*. Just as important, she required them to journal about their experiences. In the process and through the years, her kids' lives were transformed. Against the odds, she helped 150 students learn, grow, and graduate. Most went to college. Some became teachers themselves.

We all have more power than we sometimes give ourselves credit for. According to Stanford University psychology professor Albert Bandura, this power comprises four properties that help us achieve our goals.

1. *Intention*. We can imagine a better reality than the one we're currently experiencing. And we can work with others and within our circumstances to achieve it.
2. *Forethought*. By visualizing the future, we can govern our behavior in the present and give purpose and meaning to our actions.
3. *Action*. We have the ability to act on our plans, to stay motivated, and to respond in the moment to remain on course.
4. *Self-reflection*. We not only act; we know we act. That means we can evaluate how we're doing, make adjustments, and even revise our plans.[5]

We should think of these properties as superpowers. They're so common we rarely pause to think about them, but you can find the seed of every human accomplishment in this list. If you're attentive, you'll see them either implicitly or explicitly in all five steps of the *Your Best Year Ever* methodology.

Erin Gruwell put all of these to work in her teaching. She knew her involvement in her kids' lives could make a difference. She built a program that would accomplish her intent. She got started, made course corrections along the way, and little by little changed the lives of 150 students who would have otherwise been left behind—not to mention changing her own life.

Whatever our circumstances, we have the power to pursue a better future. Some don't buy it. They think because they can't control everything, they can control nothing. But that's only a limiting belief. By our choices we become active participants in the outcomes we experience.

During the final difficult months of the bus boycott in 1956, King preached a sermon to encourage his congregation to live hopeful lives of creative action. "Lord, help me to accept my tools," he told them to pray. "However dull they are, help me to accept them. And then Lord, after I have accepted my tools, then help me to set out and do what I can do with my tools."[6]

To show how powerful our humble tools can be, King pointed to the example of Moses, who discarded his own limiting beliefs and led his people to freedom. As we've seen, King proved the validity of his point by his own example.

The Resource Question

Gruwell's story also reminds us to avoid limiting our goals to our current resources. Resources are never—and I mean never—the main challenge in achieving our dreams. In fact, if you already have everything you need to achieve your goal, then your goal is probably too small.

When Gruwell first started out, she had no budget for books. But her students needed certain books if her plan was going to

Resources
are never
the main
challenge
in achieving
our dreams.

work. The answer? She got a second job and bought the books herself. As her goals grew, so did her need for resources. Her students wanted to bring Miep Gies, the Dutch woman whose family hid Anne Frank and her family from the Nazis, to the school to lecture. The school didn't have the budget, so the students held a series of fundraisers to make it happen. And that wasn't all. They also raised funds to bring Zlata Filipović, whose book they studied, to America.

The more they determined to step out, the more the necessary resources appeared. Their determination was the difference maker. "There is no deficit in human resources," as King said in his 1964 Nobel lecture, "the deficit is in human will."[7]

Resources are necessary, but they're never the precondition for success. The perceived lack of resources is often a benefit in disguise. In fact, dealing with constraints can trigger a cascade of unforeseen rewards. For one, they force us to rise to the occasion and give our best to the pursuit. Easy resources make for weak performance. Economist Julian Simon calls human creativity "the ultimate resource."[8] But ironically, limitations are often needed to unleash it. A lack of resources spurs resourcefulness. Limited resources build resiliency and confidence. The more times we overcome difficulties, the more capable we are of overcoming whatever comes next.

In short, an apparent lack of resources might be the most important resource we have. Our limiting beliefs keep us from seeing that. But here's a liberating truth: we live in a world of genuine abundance, a world full of the resources we need to pursue our most important goals. That doesn't mean you won't ultimately require the resources you currently lack. If your goal is big enough, you'll probably require more and different resources than you assume when you start. *But start.* A lack of resources is never a good excuse to stay put. Treat it instead as a prompt for what to tackle as the next step toward your goal.

When climbers first began making their attempt on Everest only to be rebuffed by the 28,000-foot ceiling, they'd been coming through Tibet on the mountain's northern slopes. Tibet closed to climbers after World War II. Not only were they unable to climb the full height, suddenly they couldn't even be on the mountain. Guess they should all head home, right?

Wrong. Because Edmund Hillary and other climbers believed they could break through the 28,000-foot ceiling, they used the constraint to shift their approach. After reassessing southern access through Nepal, which had previously been thought too difficult, Hillary and his expedition leader, Eric Shipton, spotted a possible route up to the top. The constraint didn't shut them down; it helped them find another way.[9]

Revise Your Beliefs

You don't have to be hemmed in by limiting beliefs. You can exchange them for liberating truths. I'd like to suggest a simple four-step self-coaching process to help you do that. It's the same method my daughter Megan Hyatt Miller and I describe in our book *Mind Your Mindset*.

Let's begin by pulling up the list of aspirations you created at the start of the book. You might even have a few more now that you've had longer to reflect. That's great. As you look at those aspirations, do any seem out of reach, impossible? That's where the process comes into play. To follow along, you can download our Full Focus Self-Coacher™ by scanning the QR code or following the URL at the end of this chapter.

IDENTIFY the Limiting Belief → **INTERROGATE** the Limiting Belief → **IMAGINE** a Liberating Truth → **IMPLEMENT** a New Strategy

First, *identify* the limiting belief associated with your reaction. I mentioned several giveaways in the last chapter. If a belief reflects black-and-white thinking, it might be a limiting belief. Same thing if it's personalizing, catastrophizing, or universalizing. Our language can help us spot trouble. Look for anything you might state in the negative or universal: *can't*, *don't*, *won't*, *never*, *always*, *constantly*, and so on.

These beliefs could be coming from past experience, the media, or your social circle. Whatever the content of the belief, no matter how true it seems, it's important to recognize that it's just an opinion about reality—and there's a good shot it's wrong. It might be something like,

- "I don't have enough experience."
- "I don't have the right experience."
- "I can't write."
- "I always quit."
- "I'm not creative."
- "I always fail eventually."
- "I'm not very good with money."
- "I'm not very disciplined."
- "I'm terrible with technology."

Let's be honest. It could be anything we think about the world, others, or ourselves. We all have our own challenges. The first time she did this exercise, Natalee, one of my Your Best Year Ever course alumni, was the tired young mom of two. She had recently quit her job and moved with her family to a new city. "One of my limiting beliefs was I just don't have enough energy," she told me. "I can't get to this because I'm trying to provide for these two little humans." That was just the start. Another of Natalee's limiting beliefs: "Maybe I am meant to be mediocre and maybe I'm just meant to have a life of insignificance."

I had a friend who was laid off from his job in his midfifties. I'll call him Greg. The Great Recession was in full swing, and he had a really difficult time getting reemployed. Over the course of three years, I started seeing this story take root in his thinking. He would say, "Well, I'm just too old." He also had two graduate degrees. Then the story became, "I'm overeducated." Greg's situation was tough, no doubt about it. But the culprit was not his age or his education. It was his beliefs about his age and education.

Whatever your story about the challenge you're facing, don't leave it floating in the air. I always find it helpful to write it down. By writing it down, you externalize it. And then you're free to evaluate it.

Second, *interrogate* the belief. This is when we evaluate whether the belief is factually accurate. As Megan and I discuss in *Mind Your Mindset*, most of what we believe is actually conjecture and guesswork. We may know one thing or another, but how that fits into the rest of what we know is often the product of interpretive leaps and assumptions. If we look at what we believe more objectively, a lot of those assumptions fall apart. It's also worth asking whether a belief is helpful. Is it enabling you to accomplish the outcomes you want, or is it preventing you from doing so?

"It was hard to see those words on paper," Natalee admitted. Until she wrote down her limiting belief, it clouded her thinking. By externalizing it, she was free to confront it. And you are too. The trick is to separate facts from stories. Facts are verifiable, objective, and certain. They are not emotions, opinions, or conclusions. You'll want to look for interpretations, causations, universals, or even changes in context. This work is essential to set the stage for imagining a new and better belief.

It's important to note that we are sometimes addicted to our limiting beliefs, just like Charlie from earlier. Maybe they offer a sense of certainty. Maybe they give a sense of drama or significance because we think we've got the world figured out. But don't get stuck there. Honest evaluation is the key to freedom.

Third, *imagine* a new, more empowering belief. If a limiting belief is simply false, you can just reject it. Sometimes this means restating a negative as a positive or making a simple swap like in my personal examples above.

That's what Natalee did. "When I saw those limiting beliefs I wrote down about me, I realized that those came from such a dark place," she said. "That's just not who I was. That was almost coming from somewhere else. Writing down the opposite of that—those liberating truths—felt so good to say something positive about myself and to begin to taste that confidence and see the hope and possibility of what I could become if I really started to believe in myself."

Sometimes, however, it's not that simple. Many limiting beliefs have a kernel of truth in them; that's what makes them so convincing. But they're not the whole truth. If a limiting belief is true or partly true, you don't have to settle for it. You can always recast or reframe the story. You might need to marshal a case, just like Bob Goff did for Don Miller. Bob took Don's limiting belief ("I'm no good at relationships") and offered him a liberating truth in exchange ("I'm good at relationships"), then pressed his case with supporting examples.

Negativity in the media provides another source of limiting beliefs. Yes, there's a lot of bad news out there. But it's only part of the picture. Against what the pundits say, evidence shows the world is improving in a number of key areas:

- World life expectancy continues to rise.
- Pay and college degrees awarded to women continue to rise.
- The number of annual hours worked continues to fall.
- The number of democracies in the world continues to rise, while the number of autocracies declines.
- The number of people enslaved around the world continues to fall.
- Violent crime rates continue to fall.
- The number of wars continues to decrease.
- The number of trees in the world continues to grow.
- Deaths from natural disasters began a sharp decline in the 1960s and remain low.

The list goes on.[10]

In response to Greg, who blamed his unemployment on his age, I pointed to the fact that older workers often have assets employers covet and which are perfectly suited for entrepreneurial environments, including life experience, intellectual capital, and deep social networks. Researchers at Duke and Harvard studied start-ups earning at least $1 million and discovered the founders' median age was thirty-nine.

"Twice as many were older than 50 as were younger than 25," says Vivek Wadhwa, who led the research team. "In a follow-up project, we studied the backgrounds of 549 successful entrepreneurs in 12 high-growth industries," he adds. "The average and median age of male founders in this group was 40, and a significant proportion were older than 50."[11] Age has its advantages.

And it's the same with youth. Early in my career I felt I was too young to succeed, and I hear people say similar things all the time. But it's a convenient excuse. Some of the most energetic and effective business owners I've ever coached are in their late twenties and thirties. I'll come back to Natalee's entrepreneurial story later, but she's in the same boat. Another friend, who's not even thirty, owns multimillion-dollar online properties and nearly a hundred convenience stores and gas stations. If you think your age is the problem, your imagination is working against you. It's a limiting belief that age defines your potential for success in your endeavors. The meaning we ascribe to age? Totally arbitrary.

When we obsess over what's wrong, we miss what's right. It skews our view and blinds us to opportunities all around us. Perhaps you think, *I'm not a details person*. Fine. Is being a details person necessary? You could accept that it is and stall out. Or you could reframe it and say something like this: "I'm not a details person, but I can always collaborate with someone who is or outsource the details."

If you think, *I'm too old to be considered for that job opportunity*, you might say, "I have more experience than other candidates." Conversely, if you think, *I'm too young for that job*, you might say instead, "I've got more energy and enthusiasm than other candidates." Consider the difference that perspective makes in a job interview. The old belief holds you back; the new one gives you a foothold for real progress.

You might not fully buy into the new belief at first. That's fine. Try it on. It may feel awkward, like putting on a coat that's too big. But if you keep telling yourself the truth, it will eventually fit and you'll get more comfortable with it. Our limiting beliefs won't immediately vanish once we start "treating" them, though; they require ongoing attention. They can sneak in when we're on a streak or in a slump. That's why I suggest using your Self-Coacher whenever you feel you're getting off track. Every time an unhelpful belief crops up, interrogate it and imagine a more empowering truth. And let me sneak in a fourth step. *Implement*. None of the previous steps matter unless you act on your new plan.

What Are Your Limiting Beliefs?

So, let me ask you: What are your limiting beliefs? They could be beliefs about the world, others, or yourself. What are the stories and expectations that prevent you from living the kind of life you want, the kind of life you were meant to live?

I encourage you to go through the Self-Coacher with a handful of your limiting beliefs. If you're looking for additional resources to overcome limiting beliefs, I recommend our book *Mind Your Mindset*. Not only do Megan and I explain why limiting beliefs are so prevalent, we also go in-depth about interrogating them and imagining new liberating truths.

You have what it takes. Upgrading your beliefs is the first step toward experiencing your best year ever. The next step is to get resolution on the past so you can move confidently into the future.

Download Your Full Focus Self-Coacher™
BestYearEver.me/SelfCoacher

EXAMPLES OF LIMITING BELIEFS VS. LIBERATING TRUTHS

LIFE DOMAIN	LIMITING BELIEF	LIBERATING TRUTH
Body	"I don't have the stamina to play tennis."	"I can bolster my stamina through high-cardio workouts to play tennis."
Mind	"I don't have time to regularly read."	"I can listen to audiobooks while I am driving to and from work."
Spirit	"I'm just one person and can't make a real difference."	"I can make a big difference in the life of one person I choose to invest in."
Love	"I am terrible at giving my spouse gifts."	"I can pay attention to my spouse's interests and likes and keep a running list of gift ideas throughout the year."
Family	"I never remember anyone's birthday."	"I can use my phone's calendar to remind me of my family's birthdays."
Community	"I can't help that the green spaces in the city are disappearing."	"I can plant and maintain a community garden for all to enjoy."
Money	"I'll never get out of debt."	"I can learn to budget and start putting a regular amount toward paying off my debt every month."
Work	"I can't speak up at a table with my superiors because they know more than I do."	"I can prepare some topics to have on hand to contribute to the conversation."
Hobbies	"I can't golf worth anything."	"There are plenty of resources I can find online to improve my game."

STEP 1

ACTION PLAN

1 Recognize the Power of Your Beliefs

"Our thoughts determine our lives," as the Serbian monk Thaddeus of Vitovnica said. Both positively and negatively, your beliefs have tremendous impact on your experience of life. Recognizing that fact is the first stage in experiencing your best year ever.

2 Confront Your Limiting Beliefs

We all have limiting beliefs about the world, others, and ourselves. Four indicators that you're trapped in a limiting belief are whether your opinion is formed by:

- Black-and-white thinking
- Personalizing
- Catastrophizing
- Universalizing

One tip for noticing is listening to your language. It's also important to identify the source of your limiting beliefs, whether it's past experience, the news media, social media, or negative relationships.

3 Upgrade Your Beliefs

Download a copy of the Full Focus Self-Coacher by scanning the QR code or following the URL at the end of chapter 3. Or get a notebook, journal, or your *Full Focus Planner* and draw three lines down the sheet so you have four columns. Now use this four-step process to swap your limiting beliefs for liberating truths:

1. IDENTIFY your limiting belief. Upgrading your thinking starts with awareness, so take a minute to reflect on what beliefs are holding you back. In the left-hand column, jot down the belief. Writing it down helps you externalize it.
2. INTERROGATE the belief. Evaluate how the belief is serving you. Is it factually accurate? Is it the only way to see the situation? Is it empowering? Is it helping you reach your goals? Is it true? In the middle column, write down what's wrong with the limiting belief.
3. IMAGINE a new, more empowering belief. Sometimes you can simply flip the limiting belief on its head. Try stating the negative as a positive. Other times, you might need to build a case against it or look at your obstacles from a better angle. What might be truer or more helpful in pursuing your aspirations? In the third column, write down a new liberating truth that corresponds to the old limiting belief.
4. IMPLEMENT a new strategy. Finally, identify your next steps based on the new story you've created. How will you move forward?

STEP 1

STEP 2

STEP 3

STEP 4

STEP 5

COMPLETE the PAST

Remember Uncle Rico from the movie *Napoleon Dynamite*? In his middle age, he's got nothing to show for his life. But when he hears about Napoleon's mail-order time machine, he gets wistful. "Ohhhh, man, I wish I could go back in time. I'd take state," he says.

His whole life is framed by the disappointment of not getting his chance to win in high school football. "Coach woulda put me in fourth quarter. We would've been state champions," he says. "No doubt in my mind."[1]

We all know people stuck in the same kind of rut, don't we? That probably includes us to some degree, if we're honest. After limiting beliefs, the next most common barrier we encounter is the past. We tow it around like a trailer full of broken furniture. We can't fully consider the future because we're too tied up in what's already happened.

The reason? We're reacting to our personal histories instead of getting the closure we need to move forward, what I call completing the past. It's possible to do. We've all gone through experiences, good and bad. But, as psychologist Benjamin Hardy says, "Your past is a story. How you frame that story will largely impact your Future Self."[2]

If we can look at the past with an abundance mindset instead of one fueled by scarcity, we can frame the events of the past as working (at least on average) to our advantage, not (completely) to our detriment. When we do that, we can move more hopefully and expectantly into the future. If, on the other hand, we emphasize being wronged, missing out, or suffering one setback after another, we'll stitch together a narrative that tends to confirm our inability to succeed. Not very empowering.

Getting stuck in the past will limit your outlook of the future. I don't want that to happen to you. If it does, it'll prevent you from experiencing your best year ever. Step 2 explains how to get the resolution you need.

4

Thinking Backward Is a Must

> We drive into the future using only our rearview mirror.
>
> —MARSHALL MCLUHAN

> You should always take the best from the past, leave the worst back there, and go forward into the future.
>
> —BOB DYLAN

I've spent most of my professional life in publishing. I've worked pretty much every job in the business—marketing, editorial, management. I even spent some time in literary representation and artist management. One of my clients had a number of very successful projects under his belt, and I was setting him up for what my business partner and I hoped would be a major new deal.

I worked my tail off for about a year, focusing exclusively on this one client. Before taking his new book to publishers, my business partner and I conducted a ninety-day, thirty-city tour with our client. Turnout was fantastic. We ran between fifteen hundred and two thousand people a night. When it was all done, my team and I were exhausted. But it was worth it. Our client's existing publisher took notice and offered a preemptive two-book deal for $1 million a book. *Wow!* My partner and I were over-the-moon excited. We'd invested a lot in this deal, and it was about to pay off in a big way.

We told our client and expected an enthusiastic response. But then we couldn't get our calls returned. It was stone-cold silence. Something was up. After trying for a few weeks, I finally got a response. It was written in legalese, but the message was clear. On the verge of my biggest deal to date, I got fired.

The deal I had lined up for my client was huge, but it made him think he could land an even bigger fish. He signed with an agency that promised they could do better. Meanwhile, I was left high and dry with nothing to show for my yearlong investment. It sent me into a tailspin. I was an emotional wreck. I felt like my career was over.

Backward Thinking

Completing the past is an essential part of designing a better future. "Reasoning flows not only forward," as psychologists Daniel Kahneman and Dale Miller say, "but also backward, from the experience to what it reminds us of or makes us think about." They call this "the power of backward thinking."[1] If we're going to experience our best year ever, we need to harness the power of backward thinking for ourselves. Why?

We can't complete the past until we acknowledge what we've already experienced. As a friend once told me, "An experience is not complete until it is remembered." We can't just ignore it or wish it away. Whatever we have experienced over the last twelve months—or even further back—must be addressed. If we try to ignore it, it's just going to come back to bite us. How?

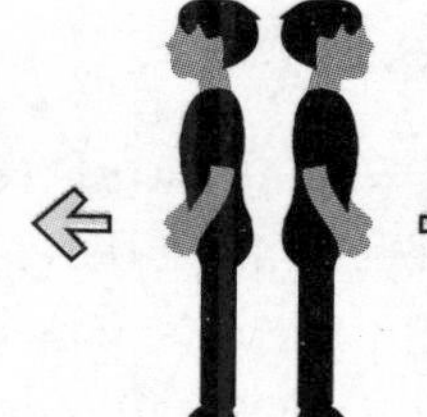

We can reason forward and back. Backward thinking allows us to learn and grow, which facilitates greater progress in the future.

Sometimes we live inside unhelpful stories we tell ourselves. Other times we nurse grievances to justify our current actions or feel unvalued because we were slighted or disregarded in some way. If we don't get resolution, we'll drag all our unfinished business into the future, and it will sabotage everything we're trying to build going forward.

Now, before going any further, I want to stress something. The process I outline next is designed to help you deal with setbacks and frustrations. It's not designed to help you deal with serious trauma. Many of us have endured some real shocks, even catastrophes. Maybe you lost a marriage. Maybe you lost a loved one. Maybe you experienced an accident, an illness, a violent attack, or the total loss of your business. Unless and until you deal with traumatic events, they can influence and even define your future in deeply unhealthy ways.

What I detail below can only get you so far. If you need to bring in outside resources, such as a therapist, I recommend you do. As Brené Brown says, that's "pure courage."[2] For the rest of us, listing our disappointments and processing them can suffice. Along with that, let me hasten to add that we must also process our successes and achievements; it's essential to note when things go well. Like Bob Dylan said, we take the best from the past with us into the future.[3]

The After-Action Review

The US Army has a helpful backward-thinking method. It's called the after-action review. First developed in 1981, it has been used ever since by America's armed forces to improve performance and get better at what they do. After an event, the goal is to understand what happened, why it happened, and how they can improve. Lots of businesses use this process, and we can use it too. This kind of backward thinking will put you in an excellent frame of mind as you get ready to design your future and experience your best year ever.

Marilyn Darling, Charles Parry, and Joseph Moore studied the after-action review process for *Harvard Business Review*. They give the example of a training battle in the California desert. I'll call the two sides Team 1 and Team 2. Team 1 was top-notch and rarely defeated. Their job was to help train Team 2 by running them through a near-life scenario. But in this case, Team 2 managed to surprise the trainers with an unforeseen attack plan. *Whoops!* Team 2 broke Team 1's defenses and left them outgunned and outmaneuvered.

Did the trainers hang their heads in shame and defeat? No. Instead, they conducted an after-action review. They studied what went wrong, what went right, and how to adjust their approach in the future. In fact, Team 1's commander called it "a good rehearsal" for upcoming engagements. Why is this important? Because completing the past is all about moving into the future. As the authors of the *HBR* study say, an after-action review is "a living, pervasive process that explicitly connects past experience with future action."[4]

I'll break down this review process into its four key stages. We'll move through each stage with several questions, and I encourage you to use a journal or notebook to jot down your answers.

Writing is a powerful tool for leveraging the benefits of backward thinking. According to a study by University of California researchers Sonja Lyubomirsky, Lorie Sousa, and Rene Dickerhoof, "Participants who processed a negative experience through writing or talking reported improved life satisfaction and enhanced mental and physical health relative to those who [merely] thought about it."[5]

Ready to begin?

Stage 1: State What You Wanted to Happen

For the military, this is pretty straightforward. Think of it as the battle plan or the object of the mission. For you, this could be your list of goals from the prior year. It could also be something less definite. Maybe it's a hope, dream, or unstated expectation.

Start by asking yourself, *How did I see the year going?* and *What were my plans, my dreams, my concrete goals, if I had any?* Don't focus on just one or two areas. Remember, our lives consist of nine interrelated domains: body, mind, spirit, love, family, community, money, work, and hobbies. It's important to get clear on what you wanted to happen across all these domains. In the case of my personal example at the beginning of this chapter, I wanted to raise my client's visibility, enhance his desirability to publishers, and land the biggest deal of my career to that point.

Blake, one of my Your Best Year Ever alumni, planned to move to New York, find a new job, and invest in a long-term relationship. But right before he took the leap, life took a turn. His girlfriend broke off their relationship while he was visiting

New York. It was a Monday. On Wednesday, his neighbor back home called to say a tree had fallen on his house.

"Fortunately, nobody got hurt," Blake said. "But they did condemn the building." If that weren't enough, his mom called that same week and said she was selling her house, which was an emotional blow because he grew up there and had a lot of attachment to the place.

"So I went from going to pursue this girl and do this new career to no relationship, homeless, and no childhood home either." If his year had been a movie, Blake said it should have been titled *I Didn't Expect It to Go That Way*.

Maybe you can relate. As you think through each life domain, don't be surprised if you start feeling uncomfortable. I can tell you from previous clients who have worked this process that you might experience profound emotion. Some people feel disappointment. Others enjoy real excitement. Some feel sad. Others get angry.

"I had so much emotional baggage around having failed achieving my goals in the past and around my health problems, and unresolved conflicts in relationships," admitted Ray, another Your Best Year Ever alum. "I never before had the emotional experience I had going through that complete-the-past exercise."

This isn't true for everyone, of course. Mileage varies, as they say. Some people feel energized by their performance in the prior year. And don't be surprised if you don't feel any significant emotion at all. The important thing is to just be aware of your feelings as you work through these four stages.

Stage 2: Acknowledge What Actually Happened

As you stated what you wanted to happen, you probably became aware of some gaps. You wanted to drive from Los

Angeles to New Jersey. Meanwhile, your car threw a rod in Arkansas. There's a distance between your desire and current reality. Some of your goals, perhaps many of them, remain unfulfilled. So ask yourself: *What disappointments or regrets did I experience this past year?*

Because these memories can be painful, it's tempting to dismiss or ignore them. But as journalist Carina Chocano says, "The point of regret is not to try to change the past, but to shed light on the present."[6]

You don't want to leave these memories hanging in the air or push them behind you like they don't matter. Both will prevent you from taking meaningful action in the present. I'll return to the subject of regret in the next chapter. I want to share some research findings that can trigger powerful personal and professional growth in the coming year. For now, it's enough to jot down your disappointments so you can begin doing business with them.

Another question to ask yourself: *What did I feel I should have been acknowledged for but wasn't?* This question was powerful for Your Best Year Ever alum James: "A lot of my limiting beliefs came from the past and the failures I had," he said. "Truthfully, they weren't big failures, but my mindset at the time was 'You're failing, you're failing, you're failing.' There were a lot of things that I wasn't acknowledged for. And I translated that into, 'Well, you must have not done well enough.'"

When he recognized that, James was able to reframe it. "No," he told himself. "You weren't acknowledged because you were in the wrong place." That realization ultimately led to renewed confidence and an important career change.

Let's face it: some version of that story happens to all of us. Maybe you're a single mom who works hard, provides for your kids, and overcomes the odds every day. Or maybe you made the heroic decision to stand for your marriage when you really felt like quitting. Maybe you committed to sacrifice part of your morning to exercise when it felt like you really didn't have the time. Whatever it is, there's real emotional power in just admitting what we wish others would have noticed and commended in our actions but maybe didn't.

Don't stop there. Ask yourself, *What did I accomplish this past year that I was most proud of?* Completing the past is not just about processing failures and disappointments. It's also about acknowledging and celebrating your wins. It's important to observe not only what went wrong but also what went right and how your beliefs and behaviors contributed to that outcome.

We often downplay this or never think to do it. But it's key to recognizing our agency and how we've overcome obstacles already. That gives us confidence for the future.

It could have been something like running a 10K or even a half-marathon this last year. Or maybe you celebrated a milestone in your job or marriage. Maybe you completed a degree or paid off the last of your student debt. Maybe you launched a new business or beat your sales targets by a significant percentage. Regardless of what it is, it's important to acknowledge what you accomplished this past year. I bet you're doing better than you give yourself credit for.

Natalee, the Your Best Year Ever alum I introduced earlier, said this exercise was "pivotal" for her. She came alive as she analyzed the positive impact she'd had on people she left in her previous job. "I realized that I had done some really amazing things," she said. "It felt good for me to acknowledge that myself. But it also felt good to acknowledge that I was moving across the country, and I was picking up my whole life. I was quitting this job that I loved, and I was doing it for my family.

It was really good that I took the time to congratulate myself on those accomplishments."

For our next question, ask, *How do the events of the past year—good or bad—ultimately serve for my benefit?* This is where we can most intentionally begin reframing our experiences into more empowering stories about our past. I'm not talking about ignoring real setbacks, hurts, or disappointments. I'm talking about choosing to imbue those experiences with beneficial meaning. How we characterize the past matters every bit as much as what actually occurred, if not far more.

"When you frame the past negatively," warns Benjamin Hardy, "your goals become reactive to and based on your past. Your goals become short term and avoidance-oriented, where you try escaping the pain of the present." On the other hand, he says, "Having a positive past depends very little on what events actually occurred. What happened to you doesn't matter as much as what story you decide to tell yourself about what happened. . . . The story you create about past events dictates what your past means to your present and to your Future Self."[7]

To finish this stage, it's useful to tease out some themes. *What were two or three specific themes that kept recurring?* These could be single words, phrases, or even complete sentences. For me, this past year was about being highly productive while protecting my margin. Not only did we launch a new book, *Mind Your Mindset*, I also set aside more time for writing and coaching clients. But it was vital for me to do so while still getting the rest and rejuvenation that makes that kind of productivity possible in the first place.

That's just me. Maybe your theme was making difficult decisions in a challenging economy. Another one could be challenging negative beliefs about your body. Or maybe it was stepping out and starting a new business. Or restoring a damaged relationship. There are as many examples as there are people.

Stage 3: Learn from the Experience

Let me go back to the story that started the chapter. When my client fired me on the verge of our biggest deal to date, it floored me. I thought I had done a great job. Besides, we had enjoyed a long-term personal relationship. I worked my tail off for about a year, focusing exclusively on this one client. But my client wasn't so impressed. He had his eye on bigger things and decided I couldn't take him there. So, without so much as a discussion, he dumped me.

In the end it was a humbling but helpful experience. I learned three important lessons. First, clients (and customers) can be fickle. I can't afford to put all my eggs in one basket. If I don't spread the risk, I might find myself in serious trouble again. Second, I learned I can't assume today's victories will be remembered or appreciated. I have to keep raising the bar. Finally, I learned I need to secure alignment from all the relevant parties up front. It turned out my client and his board had different ideas about what I was delivering. All three lessons have been invaluable over the years.

What about you? Ask yourself, *What were the major life lessons I learned this past year?* Unless we learn from our experiences, we can't grow. You've probably heard the line from the Spanish philosopher George Santayana, "Those who cannot remember the past are condemned to repeat it." If you have trouble identifying your key lessons from the year, one way to suss them out is to ask what was missing from your success. Maybe it was strategic planning—you wish you had done more of that in your business. Maybe you wish you had saved more money, spent more time with your spouse, or played more with your kids, or taken a sabbatical, or read more books. Listing these missing ingredients is an effective way to learn what went wrong and what it would take to go right in the future.

Santayana also said, "Progress . . . depends on retentiveness."[8] To retain these lessons, you'll want to distill your discoveries into short, pithy statements. That transforms your learning into wisdom to guide your path into the future.

Just for an example, here's one I wrote down a couple of years ago: "There comes a point in every experience when I'm too far in to quit but almost certain I can't finish. If I keep moving forward, I'll eventually get to the other side." That was an important life lesson for me to learn at that time, and I can pull it up when I face similar experiences today. Here's another one: "Don't overthink the outcome; just do the next right thing." Or, "I can do anything I want. I just can't do everything I want." I'm still not done learning that lesson!

You get the idea. Distill the lessons from your experiences so you don't lose them and so they can serve as tools moving forward.

Stage 4: Adjust Your Behavior

If something in your beliefs and behaviors contributed to the gap between what you wanted to happen and what actually happened, something has to change. In fact, that gap will only widen and worsen unless you pivot. It's not enough to acknowledge the gap. It's not even enough to learn from the experience. If you don't change your beliefs and how you act on them, you're actually worse off than when you started.

If I hadn't adjusted my behavior as a result of what I learned from losing my business, all that grief would have been for

Distill the lessons from your experiences so they can serve as tools moving forward.

nothing. I would have found myself in the same situation again and again. Instead, as I've progressed in my career, I've acted on those lessons and saved myself a lot of trouble as a result.

I mentioned before that businesses often use after-action reviews to improve their performance. But the improvement doesn't always happen, does it? The reason, according to *Harvard Business Review*, is that organizations drop the ball at the end. They usually don't apply what they learned, so their findings just gather dust on a shelf or get lost on a server someplace. Don't let that happen to you.

Going Forward

Despite the rough start, after finishing his after-action review, Ray said it was "the most powerful part of the course" for him. Why? "When I was done with that process, I felt so clear. It was like there were a thousand little windows open on my computer at the same time, and I was able to—*click*—close all the windows. It was very freeing."

I bet the same will be true for you. Thinking backward like this can help us learn from the past and positively build our futures. The four stages of an effective after-action review are beneficial for completing your past. But it's also beneficial to recognize that some of our greatest disappointments may lead us to our greatest possibilities for the new year. I'll cover that next.

5

Regret Reveals Opportunity

> My new rule: whenever things go wrong, wait and see what better thing is coming.
>
> —SCOTT CAIRNS

> If everything was perfect, you would never learn and you would never grow.
>
> —BEYONCÉ KNOWLES

Early in my career I was a busy executive working to make my mark in the publishing industry. Books were my world, and I loved my work. I was hungry and eager to advance. But work was only part of my life. My wife, Gail, and I started having children a few years after we got married. We had five daughters in less than ten years. As you can imagine, life was crazy.

Given the size of my family, I felt a lot of financial pressure. That, coupled with my natural ambition, was a powerful cocktail. I worked long hours, hoping I could get another promotion and the raise that came with it. For most of those years I also managed extra work on the side to meet our needs and gain financial ground.

Long story short, I often felt overwhelmed with all I had to do. I felt guilty for not spending more time at home, and I was teetering on the edge of burnout. The stakes at work were too high. But the stakes at home were higher still. Somehow I kept it all going, even through a few serious business crises. But eventually I found out that I was in danger of losing my connection with my daughters, and Gail sometimes felt like she was a single mom, widowed by all my work.

Honestly, things were touch and go at times. As I became aware of the cost my absorption with work inflicted on my family, it was like a giant regret bomb went off in my lap. Chances are good you can identify to one degree or another.

Regret is part of our "cognitive programming," according to author Daniel Pink. He recently led a massive study on regret. Pink's team asked almost 4,500 Americans many questions, but among them was how often they look back in life and wish they'd done something differently.

"Only one percent of our respondents said they never engage in such behavior," says Pink, "and fewer than 17 percent do it rarely." But what's really amazing is how universal recognizing regret seems to be. "About 43 percent report doing it frequently or all the time," he says. "In all, a whopping 82 percent say that this activity is at least occasionally part of their lives, making Americans far more likely to experience regret than they are to floss their teeth."[1]

No Autocorrect for Tattoo Needles

When I was young, the only people with tattoos were bikers, convicts, and sailors. Over the last couple of decades, that's changed in a big way. Where I live, just outside Nashville,

Tennessee, it's impossible to miss elaborate, colorful designs on full display or peeking out of shirt collars, sleeves, and trousers. And that's true all over.

According to a Harris Poll, nearly a third of American adults have a tattoo these days.[2] The percentage is higher at home. Three of my daughters have tattoos.

So far, my girls love theirs. That's true for most, but regrets are also normal. About one in four laments the decision to get a tattoo. Why? Tattoos can last far longer than the desire to get one. Beyond that, not everyone with an ink gun is Michelangelo, and tattoo needles don't come with autocorrect. Here are a few that miss the mark:

- "Never Forget God isint Finished with me Yet"
- "Everything happends for a reason"
- "Life Is a Gambee So Take the Chance"
- "No Dream Is To Big"
- "Keep Smileing"
- "Regret Nohing"

According to the Harris Poll, poor execution is one of the main reasons people regret tattoos. A website I checked had well over nine hundred examples of bungled designs, including the ones above.[3] No wonder tattoo removal is now the fastest-growing cosmetic procedure in the world.[4] And no wonder unflattering tattoos are such well-fitting symbols for regret. But that's only part of the picture.

When Brené Brown was researching the topic of regrets for her book *Rising Strong*, a friend sent her a similar example—the parents'-worst-nightmare boyfriend from the Jennifer Aniston movie *We're the Millers*, who proudly shows off his "No Ragrets" tattoo. "It's such a perfect metaphor for what I've learned," Brown says. "If you have no regrets, or you intentionally set out to live without regrets, I think you're missing the very value of regret."[5]

The *value*? One challenge most of us face in completing the past is the nagging feeling that we failed somehow. This isn't tattoos. This is existential. If you're still breathing, you're probably aware of at least one way you haven't measured up. After a little backward thinking, with help from the last chapter, that number can easily balloon to dozens, even hundreds. It can be a downer.

But this is no tragedy. Some people are a little stunned to think regret has any value at all. Our culture tends to miss it. I don't mean to minimize the pain of regret. The pain can be real and intense. The problem is how quickly we distance ourselves from it. We'd rather not live with the feeling long enough to gain the benefit. But that's a big mistake.

When it comes to experiencing your best year ever, we can leverage our regrets to reveal opportunities we would otherwise miss. Look at it the right way, and regret is a gift of God. To quote University of Michigan psychologist Janet Landman in her book on the topic, "It all depends on what you do with it."[6]

The Uses of Regret

Before we look at the benefits, let's examine one common but unhelpful use of regret: self-condemnation. "The delta between *I am a screwup* and *I screwed up* may look small," says Brown, "but in fact it's huge."[7] When we focus on ourselves instead of our performance, we make it harder to address improving next time around for the simple reason that improvement isn't the focus.

Let's say you lost your cool with one of your children or a friend. Or let's say you flubbed a report that cost your business a lucrative new client. You could go on about how bad you are as a person. That would be small comfort to your friend or coworkers and wouldn't accomplish anything as far as future behavior. Or you could identify the bad performance. By doing that, you'd be in a position not only to repair the present breach but also to prevent it from occurring again.

Self-directed regrets not only fail to help improve our performance, they sit on the evidence table in the criminal court of our minds as an ever-expanding mound of exhibits, proving all our worst limiting beliefs about ourselves. Never mind the built-in confirmation bias. We're all fallible, so if you believe you are a failure, you'll never run out of proof. Every new instance further cements the story. And since we tend to experience what we expect, as we've seen, you're likely to just get more of the same.

If, on the other hand, you believe you simply sometimes fail, you can begin evaluating what's missing in your performance and seek corrective action. There's an adage: "Success consists of going from failure to failure without losing enthusiasm." You're not a failure, so the failure you do experience creates dissonance that requires your attention to resolve.

That's what happened to me when I realized my approach to work was alienating my family. My wife and daughters mattered to me—more than my work—but my actions said otherwise. That dissonance drove me to change my approach and rebuild those relationships.

Landman identifies several benefits of regret. Three are worth mentioning here:

1. *Instruction*, which relates back to Stage 3 of the after-action review process. Regret is a form of information,

and reflecting on our missteps is critical to avoiding those missteps in the future.

2. *Motivation* to change. Landman says, "Regret may not only tell us that something is wrong, but it can also move us to do something about it." I sure felt that with Gail and my daughters.
3. *Integrity*. Regret can work in us like a moral compass, signaling us when we've veered off the path.[8]

These three reasons alone should be enough to rethink our instant dismissal of regret. When the regret bomb blew up in my life, I was able to reevaluate and reorient my priorities. Restoring my most important relationships was hard work, but without regret, it would have been impossible. I would have been oblivious to the need or resentful that others weren't pulling their weight.

Regret forced me to own my part in the failure and correct it, and the relationship with my daughters has never been better than it is today. But there's even more going on here.

The Opportunity Principle

Several years ago, a pair of researchers from the University of Illinois ranked people's biggest regrets in life. Neal J. Roese and Amy Summerville combined the results of multiple studies and subjected them to fresh analysis, along with conducting additional studies of their own.

Family, finances, and health all made the list, but the six biggest regrets people expressed were about education, career, romance, parenting, self-improvement, and leisure. Notice how these high-regret areas correlate closely to the nine life domains

I outlined at the start of the book. If your LifeScore was low in any particular domain, welcome to the human drama. You're not alone.

Roese and Summerville mapped a three-stage process of action, outcome, and recall. In the first, we take steps toward a goal. In the second, we experience the result of our effort. If unsuccessful, we often trigger regret. Where it gets interesting is Stage 3, recall.

The researchers found that "feelings of dissatisfaction and disappointment are strongest where the chances for corrective reaction are clearest."[9] Regrets, in other words, don't just flow backward like a blocked sewer pipe, oozing bad past experiences. They also point forward to new and hopeful possibilities. They call their finding the Opportunity Principle, and it's almost 180 degrees from our typical assumptions.

Regrets don't only goad us toward corrective behavior; studies show we also tend to feel regret the strongest when the opportunity for improvement is at its greatest. No one does well under a crushing burden of regret. Thankfully, our minds have natural processes like reframing to take the weight off, especially when there's little chance to fix the situation. We've recognized that since forever. It's where we get folk wisdom like "time heals all wounds."

What we haven't always recognized is that regret sometimes dogs our heels precisely because it's signaling a chance to improve our situation, whether that's going back to college, changing careers, or repairing relationships.

I'm going to fictionalize some of the details, but a woman I know—let's call her Jen—fell out of touch with her family. Feeling trapped in a controlling relationship, she had bought into several limiting beliefs her significant other had told her. She didn't believe she had any skills to hold a steady job. She was told and then believed that she was bad at math and therefore couldn't handle the couple's finances. She was also told that her family had been negative toward her partner and that she should hold a grudge against them and not keep in contact.

These toxic beliefs burdened her. Holidays were sad and lonely. The COVID-19 pandemic created a perfect environment for her partner to take advantage of her mindset about herself and her potential. When yet another Christmas came and went without seeing her parents or siblings, Jen started to recognize the feeling of regret.

One day, after a particularly heated argument with her partner, she picked up her phone and instinctively dialed her childhood home phone number. Her mother answered, and Jen broke down in tears.

"Hearing my mother's voice brought this wave of regret I had suppressed for years," Jen shared. "I was led to believe my family were the bad people of my life's story. That they were to blame for all my struggles."

Jen tearfully recounted her restorative conversation with her mom that ultimately became the catalyst for Jen leaving her rotten relationship, moving in temporarily with her sister, and rebuilding her relationship with her family. Freed from the influence of her partner, Jen also found it easier to combat the limiting beliefs she'd accepted.

Jen did what Daniel Pink says we should all do: optimize regret.[10] Rather than remaining under the weight of her situation, she allowed that feeling of regret to propel her toward reconciling with her family. It's a perfect picture of the Opportunity Principle in action, and I'm sure Jen's tug of regret resonates with all of us in one area of our lives or another. Roese and Summerville say, "Regret persists in precisely those situations in which opportunity for positive action remains high."[11]

This points to at least one reason Landman subtitled her book *The Persistence of the Possible*. Regret is a powerful indicator of future opportunity.

A Road Sign, Not a Roadblock

The Opportunity Principle is a game changer. Think about your LifeScore. In which domains did you score the lowest? Maybe your social life, hobbies, and spiritual development. Or maybe your career path or financial health. Whatever those domains are, it's time to rethink regret. Instead of a roadblock to progress, think of it as a road sign pointing the way forward.

Earlier in this chapter, I quoted Daniel Pink saying that regret is part of our "cognitive programming." The positive features of regret are actually baked right into our neurobiology. Brain scans locate the experience of regret above our eyes in the medial orbitofrontal cortex. When that portion of the brain has

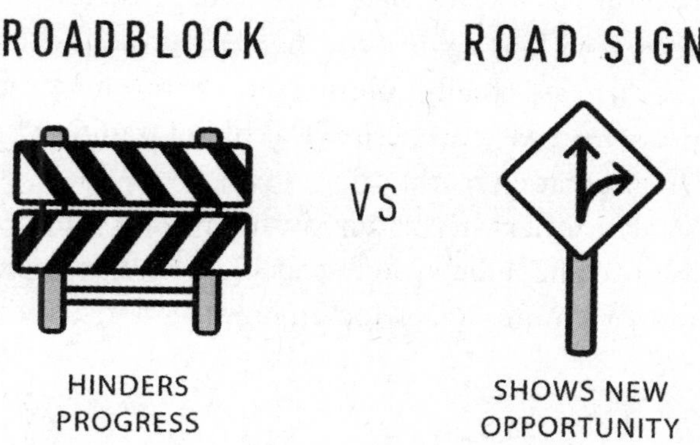

We can treat regret like a roadblock to our progress—or a road sign that points the way to a better future.

been damaged, patients not only lack feelings of regret, they are unable to correct behavior that would trigger regret in a healthy person.[12]

In other words, the fact that we feel regret at all is evidence that we have what it takes to make positive change in our situations, no matter how dire they might seem. The only people with no hope are those with no regrets. Thankfully, as Pink's regret study shows, that's probably not many of us at all. If you feel regret, there's still a possibility of rectifying the issue, or at least growing from the experience.

"Regret feels bad, yes," affirms Neal Roese, "but it also forces the individual to look inward, to reassess the assumptions and patterns of the past." He points to value in "experiencing regret deeply, listening to what these emotions tell [us], what they reveal about [our] deepest wishes, then acting quickly on these newfound insights."[13]

What if your greatest frustrations from the previous year were actually pointing you to some of your biggest wins in the next? What if regret isn't reminding us of what's impossible but rather pointing us toward what is possible? Instead of seeing our regrets as working against the chance to grow and improve, we can see them as actually pointing the way toward the growth and improvement we most desire. Talk about trading a limiting belief for a liberating truth!

As we take the next step in our journey toward your best year ever, I want to encourage you to stay in a frame of possibility. And I have one more suggestion on how to do it.

The only people with no hope are those with no regrets.

6

Gratitude Makes the Difference

It is only with gratitude that life becomes rich.

—DIETRICH BONHOEFFER

Unless you are utterly exploded, there's always something to be grateful for.

—SAUL BELLOW

By his retirement in 2022, Duke University's Mike Krzyzewski ranked in the top spot for the winningest coach in college basketball. His players had won more than 1,200 games, five national championships, and dozens of lesser titles and championships. And I know his secret.

Before their 2015 tournament, Coach K and his players and coaches wrote the names of people who had helped them on a ball. "We told the team, 'We are going to have this ball with us on our way through this tournament, and we would like for you to write on the ball the names of people who have made it possible for you to be here—people who mean something to you,'" Coach K revealed in an interview with journalist Don Yaeger.

The players took the ball everywhere. "Players started carrying the ball around—to team meals, on the plane, at practices, in the locker room," he said. "Some of the guys even slept with it—had it right there with them in their rooms." After the team took the prize, everyone with a name on the ball received a note saying, "Thanks. You were with us every step of the way."[1]

The ball kept gratitude at the center of their game. And it gave them the winning edge. Why?

The Gratitude Advantage

For a long time, researchers have questioned the connection between gratitude and our ability to strive for important goals. There's an unproven but widely held assumption that gratitude can leave people feeling complacent. *If I've got enough*, the thought runs, *then maybe I don't need to achieve more*. You can see how that would be a goal killer. Why set goals when life's good as is? But that didn't sound right to researchers Robert Emmons and Anjali Mishra.

Emmons and Mishra crafted a study comparing grateful and nongrateful goal striving. They had participants keep a gratitude journal, as well as provide a list of goals they hoped to reach over a two-month period. Ten weeks later, Emmons and Mishra checked back and found the grateful participants were significantly closer than others to achieving their goals. Gratitude doesn't make us complacent, Emmons and Mishra say. Instead, "gratitude enhances effortful goal striving."[2]

There are several reasons for this, and they all have to do with resiliency. I don't know about you, but I've never met anyone who wins at very much for very long without resiliency. I call these combined reasons the gratitude advantage, and it applies not only to basketball players but also to leaders, lawyers, entrepreneurs, parents, pastors, doctors . . . anyone.

The first way gratitude makes us resilient is that it keeps us hopeful. Gratitude is a game of contrasts. Our circumstances look a certain way; then something happens to improve them. Gratitude happens when we take notice of the distance between the two states. Suddenly, we have something to be thankful for.

That process teaches us something critical about life. While our circumstances might be bad, they can also be better. And our stories prove it to us again and again. Gratitude keeps us positive, optimistic, and able to keep coming back for more when life throws obstacles in our way. It's a key antidote to the kind of scarcity thinking I talked about earlier. By recognizing abundance, expressing gratitude actually nudges us away from

GRATITUDE

KEEPS US
HOPEFUL

IMPROVES OUR
PATIENCE

REMINDS US WE HAVE
AGENCY

EXPANDS POSSIBLE
RESPONSES

Gratitude has many variables, but one often overlooked benefit is boosting our resiliency.

scarcity and toward more abundance thinking. Less Charlie, more Amy.

Next, gratitude reminds us we have agency. As we discussed earlier, we have the power to act and effect change in our lives. Think back to the four properties of this power identified by Albert Bandura: intention, forethought, action, and self-reflection. Gratitude can play a part in optimizing each, especially self-reflection.

Because gratitude involves giving thanks for what others have done for us, this might seem counterintuitive. But that's an illusion. You know what they say about unopened gifts. If we didn't use our agency to receive and act on what others have done for us, we wouldn't have benefited.

Coach K and his players never would have made it to the tournament without the names on that ball, but they still did the blocking, shooting, and rebounding. And because of what they were already doing with the gifts others had given, they knew they could keep blocking, shooting, and rebounding all the way to the championship.

Gratitude also improves our patience and perseverance. A lot of times we take the easy way out because we're impatient. Achieving big goals takes time and effort. We're apt to cut corners or bail when we face difficulties. Thankfully, gratitude can keep us in the game.

David DeSteno of Northwestern University led a study in which participants were asked to recall an event that made them feel grateful, happy, or neutral.[3] After writing about it, they reported their mood and made a series of financial decisions. If they wanted, they could take a cash reward at the end of the session or receive a larger amount by check in the mail at a later date. The grateful were happy to wait for the bigger payout. "On average, we increased people's financial patience by about 12 percent," says DeSteno. "Imagine if you could increase people's savings by that much."[4]

Finally, gratitude expands our possible responses. Gratitude moves us into a place of abundance—a place where we're more resourceful, creative, generous, optimistic, and kind. When we're operating from a place of scarcity, we are more likely to be reactionary, closed-minded, tightfisted, gloomy, and even mean.

Researchers tell us that positive emotions like gratitude "broaden one's thought-action repertoire, expanding the range of cognitions and behaviors that come to mind. These broadened mindsets, in turn, build an individual's physical, intellectual, and social resources."[5] In other words, they make us more resilient. Psychologists and other practitioners typically refer to this as the "broaden-and-build theory." But most of us know this from practical experience. We feel better, perform better, and respond to life's ups and downs better when we're grateful.

"Gratitude helps people be more future-oriented and exhibit more self-control," says DeSteno, citing several studies. "And, unlike willpower, gratitude doesn't require much effort—people seem to enjoy expressing it."[6] Similarly, Emmons and Mishra conclude after looking at several different studies on gratitude that "the evidence strongly supports the supposition that gratitude promotes adaptive coping and personal growth."[7]

Attorney John Kralik provides a wonderful picture of this. At the close of a recent year, he was struggling. His law firm was failing, he was facing a second divorce, and he was living in a cramped apartment. Worse, he feared losing touch with his young daughter.

While hiking in the mountains, Kralik had a moment of discovery. He heard the message, "Until you learn to be grateful

Gratitude has the potential to amplify everything good in our lives.

for the things you have, you will not receive the things you want."[8] It's a simple realization, and frankly not that remarkable; what made the difference is what he did next. On that day, he decided to write a thank-you note every day for the next year.

The effect on his life was immediate. His perspective shifted, and he realized, despite his low circumstances, that he was very blessed. That change in attitude transformed his life. His finances improved, his law practice began to thrive, and he ended the year much healthier and happier. That's the power of having a grateful heart.

Disciplines of Gratitude

Regardless of our individual circumstances, we all can point to assets, blessings, and gifts in our lives. Yes, there are a million things we don't have. But there are a million we do. Whatever our past, if we can see it through the lens of gratitude, we will discover that our present is full of more than we can possibly ask or imagine. Gratitude has the potential to amplify everything good in our lives. It's the best remedy I know for the affliction of scarcity thinking and the best way to cultivate a mindset of abundance.

When I asked successful business and thought leaders how they prepared to reach their goals in the coming year, several told me gratitude gave them an edge. Some mentioned setting aside special time to reflect and express gratitude for all the positive they experienced.

"I enjoy taking the Thanksgiving holiday to be thankful for all the positive things that happened over the past year, as well as assess how I can change my perspective on the negative things that happened to a healthy one," award-winning podcaster Erik Fisher told me.[9]

Based on both what I've read in the research and my own experience, I believe gratitude is fundamental for achieving our goals. "If you do it daily," Jon Gordon, author of the bestselling book *The Energy Bus*, told me, "you'll notice incredible benefits and major life change."[10]

To leverage the gratitude advantage in my own life, I've benefited from adopting these three disciplines.

1. I start and end the day with prayer. Instead of bookending the day with what I failed to get—sleep or accomplishments or whatever—I try focusing on the blessings I do have and expressing them in prayer.
2. I practice thankfulness. Before I get caught in endless comparisons, I express gratitude for the gifts I do have. I find prayer before meals gives me several natural points in the day to do this.
3. I journal my gratitude. Journaling is useful for many things, but expressing and capturing our gratitude is certainly one. Not only do I have the in-the-moment benefit of focusing on the good, I've recorded it for later reflection, for those times when things don't feel like they're going as well as I had hoped.

Jeremy Adam Smith, editor of *Greater Good* magazine, offers several specific suggestions that can augment these. He recommends savoring positive experiences, recognizing the gift of other people and of our interconnectedness, getting specific when expressing thanks—the finer the detail, the better the evidence that you truly noticed and appreciated—and being grateful for things that don't go the way you hope or expect.

This last one is important, as Smith says, because it "can help us turn disaster into a stepping-stone."[11]

If all of this sounds like advice your mother might have given you, then your mother's wisdom tracks with the most recent findings of social scientists, psychologists, and others; all of Smith's recommendations are grounded in research conducted and coordinated by the Greater Good Science Center at UC Berkeley.

That said, gratitude exercises like these don't always work for everyone. What if you struggle to find a deep sense of gratitude? If that's true, there's nothing wrong with you. It can be normal for at least a couple of reasons. One is that we're sometimes in the midst of a moment when gratitude is hard to manage—say, controversy, anger, or resentment. Work on that first. Or find something outside those feelings to be grateful for.

The other reason we might find it hard to sense gratitude in our lives is that the wonder and mystery of it all has become so ordinary. What once delighted and surprised us can later feel rote and predictable.

Psychologist Timothy Wilson calls this the "pleasure paradox": we experience something wonderful and try to understand it so we can experience it more often, but once we understand it, we take the edge off the wonder. The way around the pleasure paradox is something he calls the "George Bailey technique."

In the movie *It's a Wonderful Life*, George Bailey decides the world is better off without him. But the angel Clarence intervenes and shows him an alternate story line, and it turns out a world without him is worse off by far. So how does it work off the silver screen?

"In our research we ask people to mentally subtract from

their lives something they cherish," says Wilson. In one study, Wilson and his colleagues compared people instructed to imagine never meeting, dating, and marrying their spouses with those instructed to simply retell how they met, dated, and married.

"Those in the George Bailey condition . . . reported greater happiness with their relationships than did the people randomly assigned to tell the story of how they had met their spouses." The difference was the alternate story line. Imagining something good never happening "made it seem surprising and special again, and maybe a little mysterious," according to Wilson.[12]

The Future Is Bright

The truth is, as attorney John Kralik discovered, that you will never have more of what you want until you become thankful for what you have. Ingratitude creates instant victims in our culture of scarcity. But giving thanks for outrageous abundance inoculates us from the sense of fear, failure, and discontent we sometimes experience and instead creates a path toward success, joy, and fulfillment.

I don't want you to think or to plan your year out of a place of scarcity. Instead, I want you to start full of gratitude. I began Step 1 with the old saying, "History doesn't repeat itself, but it rhymes." Changing the rhyme scheme starts with upgrading our beliefs, getting resolution on the past, and looking toward the future with a sense of expectation and the hope that comes from deep gratitude.

To help with that process, I recommend looking over your after-action review from chapter 4. Review your answers to those eight questions with the gratitude insights from this chapter. You can even think about some of the regrets that chapter 5 might have stoked. Gratitude, as Smith says, can offer us a stepping-stone to whatever's next.

Once you've done that, you're ready to design your future.

STEP 2

ACTION PLAN

1 Conduct an After-Action Review

To conduct an after-action review, work through these four stages: first, state what you wanted to happen; second, acknowledge what actually happened; third, learn from the experience; and fourth, adjust your behavior. I find it's effective to work through these stages by answering these eight questions:

1. How did I see the past year going?
2. What were my plans, my dreams, my concrete goals, if I had any?
3. What disappointments or regrets did I experience this past year?
4. What did I feel I should have been acknowledged for but wasn't?
5. What did I accomplish this past year that I was most proud of?
6. How do the events of the past year—good or bad—ultimately serve for my benefit?
7. What were two or three specific themes that kept recurring?
8. What were the major life lessons I learned this past year?

2 Find the Opportunity Hidden in Regret

Go back to the third question above, "What disappointments or regrets did I experience this past year?" We often feel the sharpest regret when we have the greatest chance for a positive remedy. So, ask yourself what opportunities your regrets reveal.

3 Try These Gratitude Exercises

Gratitude is not just a mood, it's a practice. These three exercises can help you get started:

- Begin and end the day with prayer.
- Practice thankfulness by expressing gratitude for the gifts you have.
- Keep a gratitude journal.

If you struggle making headway with these, try the George Bailey technique. Think of something good in your life and imagine what your life would be like without it.

DESIGN YOUR FUTURE

In 1888, on a visit to the mountains of Asheville, North Carolina, George Washington Vanderbilt II decided to build a home. He hired two famous architects, Richard Morris Hunt and Frederick Law Olmsted, to design the house and grounds. Construction began the next year and was mostly finished by 1895, when the house, known as the Biltmore, was first opened.

At 180,000 square feet, the Biltmore is considered America's largest private residence—one of the most beautiful as well. More than a million people every year line up to see its 250 rooms, 35 bedrooms, 43 bathrooms, 65 fireplaces, priceless art collection, and indoor swimming pool.[1] Meanwhile, 2,500 miles away in San Jose, California, people line up to see a very different kind of house.

Sarah Winchester bought an eight-room farmhouse in 1884 and started adding on. She built and built and built until she died in 1922. By then the rambling structure had grown to 160 rooms with a maze of passageways and no discernible master plan. The Winchester Mystery House has staircases that lead nowhere, doors that open to nothing, beautiful stained glass blocked by walls, and at least one window in the middle of the floor. In 1906, while Vanderbilt was wowing high-society guests with his dazzling achievement, Winchester admitted in a letter, "This house looks like it was built by a crazy person."[2]

But she wasn't crazy. Some say Sarah Winchester was motivated by fear, driven by spirits to never stop building. Others say she was a generous person who just wanted to keep her workers busy and employed. Whatever the motivation, the key difference between the Biltmore and Sarah Winchester's home was *design*. George Vanderbilt started with a clear vision. Sarah didn't—or if she did, it got lost along the way. And that happens to a lot of us.

Daily life consists in artfully arranging countless variables: personal hopes, family responsibilities, financial circumstances, professional demands, and more. We're building something, but we often stand back in the midst of it all and are not sure what. Look at the past year, and all of us can find some features we really like. But most will also find a few doors and hallways that lead to nowhere. It's like we're not sure what we're really trying to build.

Great results don't just happen. You don't usually drift to a destination you would have chosen. Instead, you have to be intentional, force yourself to get clear on what you want and why it's important, and then pursue a plan of action that accomplishes your objective. The Winchester Mystery House didn't have a plan—only the whim of an heiress with gobs of money—and is now an oddity cloaked with intrigue. The Biltmore sits on the other end of the spectrum. It is a lavish estate built using extensive plans, and it strives to educate the general public about architecture, art, furniture, clothing, gardens, and more.

One house boasts of intentionality and purpose. The other is a wonderful example of how working without a design produces chaos. Step 3 of our goal-achievement process is all about helping you find the clarity you need so you can design the life you want. And this, my friends, is where it gets fun.

7

Great Goals Check Seven Boxes

> Do not think or do anything without having some aim in sight; the person who journeys aimlessly will have labored in vain.
>
> —MARK THE MONK

> The reason most people never reach their goals is that they don't define them.
>
> —DENIS WAITLEY

In 2002, General Motors was determined to boost its share of the US automobile market to 29 percent, a position the company hadn't held since 1999. The company was obsessed with the number. It offered crazy purchase incentives, such as zero-interest loans, to drive sales. Executives even started wearing lapel pins with the number 29 to keep the goal front and center. But they missed it. Why?

GM blamed the competition, especially from South Korea. "If the competition would just play a little fairer, we could do it," one executive complained.[1] But analysts said GM became so focused on the goal, the company undercut its own business to attain it. Because of reckless decisions made in pursuit of their goal, the company went bankrupt several years later and became dependent on federal bailout dollars just to survive.[2]

And it's not just GM. Other organizations have fallen into similar traps. Remember Enron? Looking at these and other stories, it would be easy to conclude that goal setting is somehow counterproductive, perhaps disastrously so.[3] But that's not my take.

I've been practicing and teaching goal achievement far too long for that. I've also seen and experienced far too many successes. Not only can the pitfalls be easily overcome, but we can actually engineer our goals from the outset to avoid them entirely.

Do you still have that list of aspirations you worked on at the start of the book? In this chapter, we will transform those aspirations, resolutions, and dreams into powerful, compelling, written goals that check seven key boxes. But before I unpack this framework, I want to address why we should bother writing our goals. Since written goals are the foundation on which you build your best year ever, it deserves some explanation.

The Importance of Written Goals

There's a commonly cited Ivy League study that supposedly shows that writing down goals helps us achieve them. The problem is it's phony. And when people discover this, they sometimes think the benefits of writing down our goals are fake too.[4] But no.

Professor Gail Matthews of Dominican University of California conducted her own study not long ago and confirmed the power of writing down our goals. She recruited 267 entrepreneurs, executives, artists, health-care professionals, educators, attorneys, and other professionals from several different countries. She divided them into five groups and tracked them over several weeks. Matthews discovered, among other things, that the mere act of writing one's goals boosted achievement by 42 percent.[5] This gels with my own experience and that of people I coach.

Committing your goals to writing is foundational for success for at least five reasons. First, *it forces you to clarify what you want*. Imagine setting out on a trip with no particular destination in mind. How do you pack? What roads do you take? How do you know when you have arrived? Instead, you start by picking a destination. Clarity is a precondition for writing. (Ask any author suffering writer's block; they can't write because they're unsure what they're trying to say.)

Second, *writing down goals helps you overcome resistance*. When we go to the trouble of formulating and recording our goals, we're doing more than dreaming. We're also engaging our intellect. We're processing, self-checking, analyzing, and engaging our sense of agency and control. In a study published by the *Journal of Happiness Studies*, researchers note that composing to-do lists, creating schedules, filling gratitude journals, and jotting down thoughts about the day leave people feeling clear and resourceful and up to life's challenges.[6]

Every meaningful intention, dream, or goal encounters resistance. From the moment you set a goal, you will begin to feel it. But the emotional and intellectual engagement of writing them down helps us identify deeply with our goals and forge resolve around our desires. I'll focus on this later in Step 4.

Third, *it motivates you to take action*. Writing down your goals is only the beginning. Articulating your intention is

Writing down goals helps you overcome resistance.

important, but it's not enough. You must execute your goals. You have to take action. I have found that writing down my goals and reviewing them regularly provokes me to take the next most important action.

Fourth, *it filters other opportunities*. The more successful you become, the more you will be deluged with opportunities. In fact, these new opportunities can quickly become distractions that pull you off course. The only antidote I know of is to maintain a list of written goals by which to evaluate these new opportunities. Establishing your priorities up front equips you to intentionally avoid what some call "shiny object syndrome."

Fifth, *it enables you to see—and celebrate—your progress*. It is particularly difficult when you aren't seeing progress. You feel like you are working yourself to death, going nowhere. But written goals can serve like mile markers on a highway. They enable you to see how far you have come and how far you need to go. They also provide an opportunity for celebration when you attain them. I'll cover reasons 3–5 later in Step 5.

But to get the most from your written goals, as I said before, you need to formulate them to check certain boxes. And that's where my seven-part framework comes in. You've probably heard of SMART goals. They have five different attributes, one for each letter of the SMART acronym (Specific, Measurable, Action-Oriented, Realistic, and Timebound). My coauthor Daniel Harkavy and I used this in our book *Living Forward*. General Electric pioneered this approach in the early 1980s.[7]

Others have modified and expanded the SMART framework over the years, including me. The changes I've made to the system are based on insights from the best goal-achievement research available and are designed to drive results. Let's dive into the seven attributes of my SMARTER Goals® system now.

SMARTER GOALS

- ☑ **S**PECIFIC
- ☑ **M**EASURABLE
- ☑ **A**CTIONABLE
- ☑ **R**ISKY
- ☑ **T**IMEBOUND
- ☑ **E**XCITING
- ☑ **R**ELEVANT

We can make our goals more attainable by ensuring they check the right boxes. Write goals that are specific, measurable, actionable, risky, timebound, exciting, and relevant.

Attribute 1: Specific

The first attribute of SMARTER Goals is that they're specific. Focus is power. You can drive the same amount of water through two pipes and create greater force in one of them just by reducing its diameter. That's similar to what happens when we narrow our goals. What the studies show is that the tougher and more specific the goal, the more likely we are to engage our focus, creativity, intellect, and persistence.

Specific goals "direct attention and strategic planning," as well as "tell the performer where to concentrate and precisely what to do."[8] Vague goals don't really inspire us. And it's hard to know where to put what little effort and creativity we are willing to invest. Specific goals create a channel for our problem-solving skills, effort, and more.[9]

As humans, we're always imagining how the future might work out—how we'd like it to work out. A group of researchers dug into this phenomenon, which is called "fantasy realization theory." When our daydreams about the future harden into a firm resolve to make change, we'll have a strong commitment to complete our goals. However, fantasizing about the future without firmly committing to a goal usually keeps people stuck. In those cases, we know what we'd like to happen, but we never develop a strong drive to take action. Worst of all is when we slip into what the researchers call "mere reflections on negative reality." That's when we understand the problem but can't even imagine a solution. We're back to Charlie and scarcity thinking, and the result is anxiety, gloom, and dread.[10]

What this research tells us is that our hopes and dreams are essential for achieving goals—but only when we pair them with a strong motivation to create a specific solution. Aspirations by themselves are not enough. We have to sharpen high expectations into specific goals.

In a study out of Duke University a few years back, researchers found that people with more specific goals gained more momentum and grew in motivation as they progressed, while people with less specific goals had the opposite tendency. They lost steam along the way and reported a decline in motivation, even when they made some progress.[11] Greater goal specificity is more important than we realize. It leads to better execution and sustained drive.

To formulate a SMARTER Goal, you've got to identify exactly what you want to accomplish. For example, I could say, "Write a book," but that's too vague. What's the specific book that I want to write? In my case, I would do better to write something like "Finish writing *Time Rules*"; that's the working title of the next book I'm writing with my daughter Megan.

Here's another example: "Learn photography." Is that specific? No. What aspect of photography do you want to learn? A better goal would be "Complete Lynda.com's Photography 101 course." That's specific.

Attribute 2: Measurable

The second attribute of SMARTER Goals is that they are measurable. In other words, they have built-in criteria you can measure yourself against. This is important for two reasons.

The first is the most obvious. How do you know that you've reached the goal? It's not very helpful or inspiring to say that you want to make more money this year than last. How much more? There's a big difference between a small cost-of-living raise and driving your commissions up 30 percent. Same with getting fit. Saying you want to exercise more often doesn't do much. It's not objective. Saying you plan to go to the gym four days a week is different. When the goal is measurable, we know the criteria for success.

The second reason is that you need to be able to measure yourself against the goal. An objective target allows you to set markers and milestones along the way. That means you can chart your progress, and half the fun of goals is in the progress we make. In fact, "We experience the strongest positive emotional response when we make progress on our most difficult goals," according to psychology professor Timothy Pychyl.[12] This is especially true when we progress faster than we anticipated.[13]

Of course, measuring our progress might also show that we're lagging. But that's actually positive, too, because the gap can prompt renewed attention and action. Receiving feedback as part of measuring our goal, as one psychologist puts it, "provides the emotional punch that continually bathes the goal-setting process within emotional experiences of felt satisfaction and felt dissatisfaction."[14] We're either doing well or not—but we'll never know if the goal isn't measurable to begin with.

Attribute 3: Actionable

The third attribute of SMARTER Goals is that they're actionable. Goals are fundamentally about what you're going to do. As a result, it's essential to get clear on the primary action when formulating your goals.

If we care about our goals and want to make sure they produce results, we need to ensure we're clear on what action we're going to take. As John Doerr says, "So you're passionate—*how* passionate? What actions does your passion lead you to do?"[15]

How exactly do we gain this sort of clarity when formulating a specific goal? It may sound simplistic, but I find it's best to use a strong verb to prompt the action you want to take. You don't want something like *am* or *be* or *have*. You want a verb like *run*, *finish*, or *eliminate*.

A couple of examples: "Be more consistent in writing." Is that actionable? No. That's a state-of-being verb. But something like "Write two articles a week," or "Write 500 words each day," that's actionable. It starts with the verb *write*, and it's clear and directive about the action. Here's another: "Be more health conscious." Is that actionable? Not really. Instead, you could say something like "Walk for thirty minutes, five times a week." Much improved. Specifying the desired action provides immediate direction toward the result, coded in the language of the goal itself.

Attribute 4: Risky

The fourth attribute of SMARTER Goals is that they're a bit risky. Hear me out. Normally we talk about setting goals that are realistic. That's usually what the R in SMART refers to. But if we start by asking what's realistic, we're likely to set the bar too low.

When Your Best Year Ever alum James discovered our five-day intensive, he was making a six-figure income, but he was unfulfilled at work. He felt unrecognized for his contribution and no longer connected to the mission of the organization. He knew he needed a change. One response would have been to set a safe goal—say, addressing his problems with his employer. But James didn't do that. "I said enough's enough," he remembered. "I literally went back to my employer at the time, and I said, 'You know what? Take me off full-time salary.'" After that, he set a goal to start his own firm. James had a wife and two kids under five, but he was confident he could make a go of his own business. And he did. He even paid off $30,000 of debt he accrued when he quit his job.

The risk drove the results. Had James gone the safe route, he likely would have accomplished far less. Why? "There is a linear relationship between the degree of goal difficulty and performance," as goal theorists Edwin Locke and Gary Latham say. Looking at the results of almost four hundred studies, they conclude, "The performance of participants with the highest goals was over 250% higher than those with the easiest goals."[16] We rise to a challenge, but we hold back when it's easy.

Still, safe goals are a constant temptation for us. Psychologist Daniel Kahneman has done pioneering research on risk aversion. "We are driven more strongly to avoid losses than achieve gains," he says. "The aversion to failure of not reaching the goal is much stronger than the desire to achieve it."[17] For some, that bias is stronger than others, and it has tremendous upsides—for instance, keeping us out of trouble. But it can disserve us when we set goals, especially if we're unaware of its effect on us. Because failing feels like losing, we're tempted to set small goals we can easily reach in the name of being "realistic." We're also likely to slack off once we've reached those small goals.

I'm not saying everyone should quit their job or burn the ships. But by focusing on what's supposedly realistic, we can inadvertently trigger our natural impulse to avoid loss and end up accomplishing less than we otherwise might have. I'm not saying we should set goals that are crazy. I am saying we should set goals that stretch and challenge us. I'll have more to say on this in the following chapter.

Attribute 5: Timebound

The fifth attribute of SMARTER Goals is that they're timebound. This could involve a deadline, frequency, start date, time trigger, or streak target.

For example, if I just have the goal "Read more," it's missing a sense of urgency. It could happen over the next ten years. It could happen over the next twenty years. Even if I assume it's a New Year's resolution, so it means sometime *this year*, it's still just out there somewhere. I can put it off and stop thinking about it. But when I say I want to read two books each month, I've created not only a challenge but also a focus. Deadlines demand attention and spur action. I'd better get in motion because the clock is ticking.

Here's another example: "Acquire five new design clients." By when? "Acquire five new design clients by December 31." That's better. But here's a warning: as you're thinking about assigning deadlines, don't make them all December 31.

Distant deadlines discourage action. You'll think, *I have so much time. It's not due for another ten or twelve months*. Effort dissipates to fill time. But the reverse is also true. Short time horizons concentrate our effort. Psychologists call this the "Goal Looms Larger Effect." The tighter the deadline, the more focused and productive we tend to be.[18] A study by Locke and Latham found that workers in one field experiment were able to keep production at 100 percent even when their time was cut by 40 percent.[19]

The new deadline created huge gains in productivity—and we can experience the same sort of gains in our personal and private lives when we set near-term goals, leaving more margin for other pursuits. The main thing to watch is your bandwidth. I recommend setting eight goals per year—but only two or three major deadlines per quarter. Any more than that and your focus will suffer along with your results.

Deadlines are essential for achievement goals. But what about habit goals? I'll explain more about the differences between these two kinds of goals in chapter 9, but for now we can focus on different kinds of time keys. Deadlines don't make sense with ongoing activities. But deadlines aren't the only way to key activity to time. If we use frequency statements, start dates, time triggers, or streak targets, we can actually spur the habits we want to cultivate.

Saying "Exercise more this year" is a recipe for inaction. But saying "Run for thirty minutes at the park every weekday at 7:00 a.m., starting on January 15, for ninety days" sets you up to win. Not only does it say what kind of exercise and where you're going to do it, and not only does it say for how long, it also tells us exactly when you're going to do it, when you're going to start, and how long it'll be before you consider the habit fully installed.

Time keys for habit goals create external cues that trigger action. And they work. After telling study participants about the dangers of heart disease, researchers in the UK recommended exercise as a way to prevent it. On their own, participants intended to work out but usually forgot. They had less than a 40 percent success rate. I get it. Life's busy. But some were asked to bake a time trigger into their goal. Their success rate was better than 90 percent.[20] The time trigger helped drive the behavior they wanted to see. I'll show you how you can leverage activation triggers like these in Step 5.

Attribute 6: Exciting

The sixth attribute of SMARTER Goals is that they're exciting. They inspire you, in other words. Researchers say that we stand a better chance of reaching our goals if we are internally motivated to do so. External motivations might work for a while, but if we're not getting something intrinsic from the goal, we'll lose interest.

That was a challenge James experienced with his prior job. Others set the goals he pursued. "That was a big problem for me," he said. "I was so caught up with everyone else designing goals for me. I never took the time to design them for myself." It was a game changer for him when he finally determined to take his destiny into his own hands. "The biggest difference for me is they no longer were overwhelming goals. They were inspiring goals. When I'm inspired, I want to go." The change came down to one thing: he personally set goals that excited him.

Another Your Best Year Ever student struggled with a goal she set of getting her accounting caught up in her small business. Important? Yes. Inspiring? Not for her. As a result, she struggled to maintain momentum. We all do.

Ayelet Fishbach and Kaitlin Woolley of the University of Chicago's Booth School of Business researched New Year's resolutions. They first asked people to rate how much they enjoyed the resolutions they had set and then followed up a couple of months later. Enjoyment turned out to be a key predictor of success. But as Alice Walton reports in the *Chicago Booth Review*, "That's not how people typically choose their goals—they choose ones they feel are important. Fishbach says it's fine to go ahead and set goals that feel important, but don't compromise on pleasure entirely. 'Don't choose a New Year's resolution you don't enjoy doing.' You'll be setting yourself up for failure." Instead, Walton says, "Tap into your intrinsic motivation."[21]

Go with what excites you. If you don't find your goals personally compelling, you won't have the motivation to push through when things get tough or tedious. This is where you've got to be honest with yourself. Ask, *Does this goal inspire me?* Or, *Does it engage my heart? Am I willing to work hard to make it happen?* You might even ask if you find it fun; I usually do for at least some of my goals each year. All of these questions get at something we'll cover in the next step—finding your why. Remember, we're setting risky goals. We're going to be tempted to quit at some point. Only an exciting goal can access the internal motivation you need to stay the course and achieve your goal. More on this in Step 4.

Attribute 7: Relevant

That brings us to the seventh and final attribute of SMARTER Goals. Effective goals are relevant to your life. This is about alignment, and it comes at the end of the list because it's a good way to gut-check your goals before committing to them. Frankly, this is the main area where GM went wrong. But we can all stumble on this point if we're not careful.

If we're going to succeed, we need goals that align with the legitimate demands and needs of our lives. Are you a working

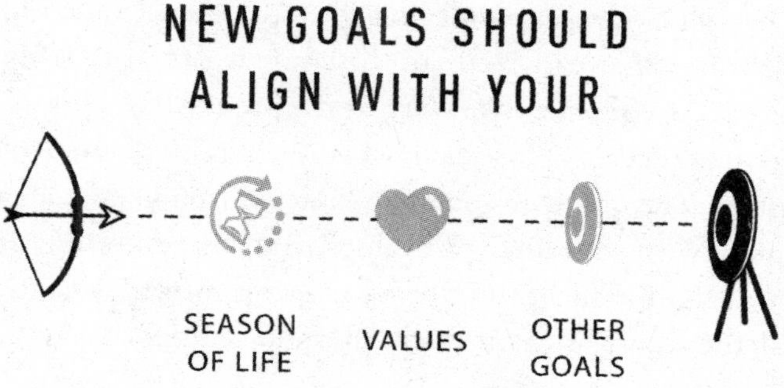

NEW GOALS SHOULD ALIGN WITH YOUR

SEASON OF LIFE

VALUES

OTHER GOALS

When a goal is relevant to our season of life, our personal values, and our other goals, we improve our odds for success.

parent with young kids? Your goals will look much different from those of an empty nester or an undergrad. Depending on your circumstances, going to med school might not be in the cards right now. Pursuing a new weekend-gobbling hobby might put unwanted strain on your family. You need to set goals that are relevant to your actual circumstances and true interests.

You also need goals that align with your values. This should be obvious, but sometimes we feel outside pressure to set goals that go against the core of who we are. The pressure could be social, professional, whatever. But you need to resist the temptation to gear your performance for others—especially if it somehow goes against your values.

Finally, you need goals that align among themselves. They must harmonize as a whole. Setting multiple conflicting goals will only create friction and frustration. If we're working against ourselves, we'll experience more heartburn than progress. That goes for setting too many goals in general.

At the start of his memoir *The To-Do List*, journalist Mike Gayle has a moment of reflection. It's his thirty-sixth birthday, and he's plagued by all the things he has yet to accomplish with his life. So he sets some goals—1,277 to be exact. Out of that list, he achieves 1,269, but the comedy of the story is the craziness his wife has to endure in the process.[22] As far as I'm concerned, reading a farce is far better than living one.

Instead, I recommend you limit yourself to eight annual goals that align with your life, your values, and your ambitions; that way you can pursue as many as two per quarter, or get a few out of the way while you work on a major goal that requires more than one quarter.

Goals of Your Own

To summarize, SMARTER Goals are specific, measurable, actionable, risky, timebound, exciting, and relevant. And now you're ready to start designing some of your own. How do you get started? I recommend you begin by pulling up your list of aspirations and your LifeScore Assessment. Your LifeScore will help you craft a set of goals that are aligned with your personal growth path.

Avoid setting more than eight goals. Any more and you'll dilute your efforts and suffer distraction. Any less and you might not stretch yourself enough. I also recommend setting a few per quarter so you can space your effort more or less evenly throughout the year.

As I've mentioned before, you'll want to include goals from several different life domains. I find that people are accustomed to setting career-related goals, but they rarely set goals in other areas of their lives. As a result, those other domains suffer, sometimes catastrophically. To jump-start your thinking, I've provided three examples below from each of the nine principal life domains.

BODY	MIND	SPIRIT
• Replace fast-food lunch with healthy meals from home each weekday. • Run 30 minutes a day, 4 days a week, at 6:30 a.m. • Choose a regular bedtime and get 8 hours of sleep per night for the next 90 days, beginning January 1.	• Read 2 books per month, starting in January. • Select 2 conferences to attend, and register by February 15. • Research foreign-language classes, and register for a beginner's Spanish class by March 1.	• Set aside 15 minutes in the morning, 6 days a week, for reading and prayer, starting January 1. • Journal for at least 5 minutes at the end of each day. • Research and find a therapist/counselor, and start regular monthly sessions by March 1.
LOVE	**FAMILY**	**COMMUNITY**
• Create a date-night profile on Netflix and identify 20 movies for weekly dates, beginning in May. • Plan 2 regular dates each month and get them on the calendar by January 15. • Pick 3 errands or tasks my spouse regularly does but doesn't enjoy. Do one each week for him/her, beginning April 1.	• Leave the office by 5:00 p.m. every weeknight to have enough time for dinner and games with the kids, starting in January. • Have the kids brainstorm 25 meals. Cook at least 1 each weekend, beginning in February. • Set aside 7 vacation days to spend with my parents at their favorite location. Schedule by March 15.	• Join an athletic club to meet new people by February 1. • Volunteer with Habitat for Humanity on a local build by July 1. • Volunteer for the City Mission, beginning in March.
MONEY	**WORK**	**HOBBIES**
• Pay off remainder of my car loan in the amount of $8,000 by August 25. • Reduce eating out to 1 meal each week, beginning January 1. • Pay down $5,000 in credit card debt by May 1.	• Launch new product by March 30. • Add 5,000 email subscribers to our database by June 15. • Quit job and launch new business by October 1.	• Attend a 12-week painting class, starting April 1. • Visit 2 new restaurants each month for the rest of the year. Make a list by January 30. • Research 12 of the best comedies ever filmed, and watch 1 each month, beginning in January.

You'll notice that some of these goals are achievements and some are habits. In chapter 9, I'll point out how to leverage the differences between the two types of goals.

To help you with your own, I've also included a series of fill-in-the-blank goal-setting templates in the back of the book. These templates will ensure that you check all seven boxes of the SMARTER system. I designed these templates for my *Full Focus Planner* to integrate several key aspects of goal achievement so you can experience your best year ever.

8

Seriously, Risk Is Your Friend

> People don't brag about going up a grassy slope. They brag about going up Everest.
>
> —PENN JILLETTE

> The comfort zone is a nice place, but nothing grows there.
>
> —CAROLINE CUMMINGS

Most of us have heard the popular story of the first marathon. After the Athenians defeated Persian invaders at the battle of Marathon in 490 BC, a messenger ran twenty-six miles to share the exciting news. In his book *The Road to Sparta*, ultramarathoner Dean Karnazes shares the real story, and it's far more compelling. The runner, whose name was Pheidippides, actually ran more than 150 miles all the way from Athens to Sparta—and then back again—before the battle. And Karnazes says the same runner might have run the final stretch after the victory at Marathon for a total of more than 325 miles!

That might sound far-fetched, but Karnazes then recounts the story of a British Air Force commander named John Foden. In

1982, he led a small group who ran the distance from Athens to Sparta in under thirty-five hours. A year later Foden cofounded a 153-mile race retracing his steps. It's called the Spartathalon.

Karnazes ran it in 2014. As an ultramarathoner, he'd already run 350 miles nonstop. But the Spartathalon held mammoth challenges of its own, including Karnazes's determination to run the distance with only the foods Pheidippides would have eaten: olives, figs, and cured meats.[1]

Why would a person willingly go through something like that? "Western culture has things a little backwards right now," Karnazes once told *Outside* magazine. "We think that if we had every comfort available to us, we'd be happy. We equate comfort with happiness. And now we're so comfortable we're miserable. There's no struggle in our lives. No sense of adventure."[2] That observation applies to all of life, especially our goals. When it comes to meaningful achievement, comfort equals boredom and low engagement.

When I first heard about Karnazes several years ago, I was so inspired I made a commitment to run my first-ever half-marathon. I've run several since, though it's never easy. And that's good.

You and I should embrace discomfort for at least three reasons, whether we deliberately choose to or it simply happens to us. First, comfort is overrated. It doesn't lead to happiness. It often leads to self-absorption and discontent. Second, discomfort is a catalyst for growth. It makes us yearn for something more. It forces us to change, stretch, and adapt. Third, discomfort signals progress. When you push yourself to grow, you will experience discomfort, but there's profit in the pain.

Personal engagement, satisfaction, and happiness all come when we're gunning toward significant, risky goals. Maybe it's launching a new product, going back to college, or reviving a

When it comes to meaningful achievement, comfort equals boredom and low engagement.

struggling relationship. If dreaming about a goal that big makes you feel uneasy, you're on the right track.

How can you confirm you're heading in the right direction? I like to find out where someone's goals relate to three specific zones. I use this same technique when evaluating my own goals. The three zones are the comfort zone, the discomfort zone, and the delusional zone.

Before we tackle the three zones, I want to dispel a myth about goals and risk. As mentioned, GM isn't the only group to get in trouble with myopic goals. The worst disaster on Mount Everest happened long after Edmund Hillary and Tenzing Norgay reached the top. In 1996, a single storm claimed the lives of eight climbers. Focusing on the myopic—and fatal—goal of the climbers and their guides, critics of goal setting zeroed in on the disaster as evidence that goals can do more harm than good.[3] They can, but as we've seen, we can also overcome those problems by properly setting our goals with the seven SMARTER characteristics in mind.

Goal setting has been studied for decades, and the results for improved performance are overwhelmingly positive. "There have been more than 1,000 academic experiments in goal-setting of which over 90% have produced positive results," reports the *Economist*, citing data from goal-research pioneer Gary Latham.[4] The goal critics raise important caveats, and we should factor in their insights to proceed wisely. But we should also proceed confidently as we rise to the challenge of our ambitious goals.

The Comfort Zone

We all have dreams for a better future. We set goals for improving our health, our family and friendships, our finances, our work lives, and more. When we start dreaming about the future, however, our aspirations can feel too fragile and too far away. We jump ahead of ourselves and start worrying about how we're going to achieve those goals. Then, because we let the *how* overshadow the *what*, we downgrade our aspiration. We don't see how we can accomplish more, so we throttle back our vision, convinced our goals must be "reasonable" or "realistic." We aim low. We settle for less. And what we expect becomes our new reality.

But the old adage is true. Nothing ventured, nothing gained. Chicago architect Daniel Burnham said it this way in 1907: "Make no little plans. They have no magic to stir men's blood and probably will not themselves be realized. Make big plans, aim high in hope and work."[5] The science backs him up. As we've discussed before, goal researchers have documented a strong, direct relationship between the difficulty of our goals and the likelihood we'll achieve them—not to mention greater motivation, creativity, and satisfaction.

For a goal to matter, it has to stretch us. That means it has to stand somewhere outside our comfort zone. If you know exactly how to attain the goal, it's probably not far enough.

I once watched a documentary about amateur ultramarathoners who were running more than six hundred miles across four different deserts.[6] One of the runners had done only a few small races before but decided to sign up. What's instructive is why. He'd never done anything like that before, he said, but he knew he'd figure it out once he committed. I'm not saying you need to sign up to run hundreds of miles in four of the world's most inhospitable places. But if you have what you need at this very moment to achieve your goal—in other words, if you can easily imagine completing the challenge—it's probably not challenging enough to be compelling.

I quoted magician and TV personality Penn Jillette at the top of the chapter: "People don't brag about going up a grassy slope. They brag about going up Everest." He said that when discussing his noticeable weight loss, making more than 100 pounds vanish from his 330-pound frame in just three months!

How'd he do it? By switching to a vegan diet with little processed food, no sugar, and extreme intermittent fasting. Before you sign up for his regimen, note his own caveat: "My first tip is this: 'If you take health advice from a Las Vegas magician, you are an idiot.'"[7] Specifics aside, what stuck with me when reading Jillette's explanation was that he struggled to control his weight using easier means. "I realized that the only way that I can accomplish anything is if it's hard," he said. "Things that are easy to do, I don't do. There's just no sort of psychological desire to do that—I just don't enjoy that."[8] It might sound surprising, but the research is on his side.

We know from the science of goal achievement that rising to the inherent risk of a goal creates huge emotional gains for us. "When goals are set too low, people often achieve them, but subsequent motivation and energy levels typically flag, and the goals are usually not exceeded by very much," according to Steve Kerr and Douglas LePelley of Chancellor University. But, they say, "difficult goals are far more likely to generate sustained enthusiasm and higher levels of performance."[9] In other words, we get more out if we put more in.

Let's say you're the sales manager of a small manufacturing plant. You've been growing at 5 percent a year, and this year you're going to set your growth goal at 6 percent. Is that going to heighten performance, engage your creativity, or up your enthusiasm? No way. Small goals just aren't very compelling. If we want to win, we need to get beyond our natural urge to play it safe; we need to jump outside our comfort zones and set some risky goals. Now imagine if that growth goal was more like 20 percent. Delivering that result will require more from you than you currently know how to manage. That's when growth happens.

Or take a personal instead of a professional example. If you've done a weekly newsletter for a whole year with subscribers who count on you delivering your message on time, why not push yourself to add a major extra weekly feature on top of your regular issue? The idea with a risky goal is to leap out of your comfort zone and into your discomfort zone. Playing it safe won't reap the same kind of rewards.

The Discomfort Zone

You've probably already experienced discomfort zone benefits to some extent before. Maybe it was learning a new skill, meeting a new person, or taking on a challenge you'd never done before. We don't often enjoy these things when they are happening, but looking back, we have to admit: the really important stuff of life happens outside our comfort zone. This is where the growth happens, where the solutions are, where fulfillment resides. But instead of encountering this retrospectively, we can engineer these experiences by intentionally embracing goals with greater levels of risk baked in.

In her book *The Upside of Stress*, Kelly McGonigal shares the story of Stanford University professor Alia Crum. As a grad student pulling an all-nighter in a basement room of the psychology department at Yale, Crum startled from a knock at the door. As it opened, a tech peered in, sized up the situation, and said, "Just another cold, dark night on the side of Everest." Crum had no time to acknowledge him or reply; he shut the door and shuffled on.

A couple of weeks later, Crum found herself returning to the man's words. When climbing Everest there are going to be some miserable times, she realized, just like she felt when working all night alone toward her degree. Crum chided herself, "But what did you expect? You're climbing Everest."

Everyone has an Everest that daunts them—dares them even—to reach the peak. At the time, Crum's Everest was her dissertation. But we all have our own version. There are times we are convinced we won't succeed. "But what," asks McGonigal, "is a worthwhile goal if it's not important enough to spend weathering a few cold, dark nights on the side of Everest?"[10]

What's fascinating is that by choosing daunting, difficult goals, we rise to the challenge with all the ingenuity and resourcefulness required. General Electric CEO Jack Welch calls this "bullet train thinking." He took the name from a revolution in Japanese transit. Traveling by rail from Tokyo to Osaka once took more than six hours. This slowed down business, and executives wanted the time cut. But they didn't establish "realistic" reductions in time, say, bringing the trip under six hours. Instead, they wanted to cut it in half. To meet the goal, engineers scrapped conventional solutions, rethought the entire problem, and revolutionized Japanese transit in the process.[11]

Importantly, the engineers didn't quite halve the time. But they got close, and certainly closer than if they had set a less ambitious goal. "By reaching for what appears to be impossible," says Welch about the experience of pursuing difficult goals at GE, "we often actually do the impossible; and even when we don't quite make it, we inevitably wind up doing much better than we would have done."[12] These "stretch" goals at GE weren't make-or-break. Executives used them to drive creative thinking and problem-solving.

For a goal to be meaningful, its attainment should lie in the discomfort zone. You'll know you're there when you start feeling emotions we normally consider negative: fear, uncertainty, and doubt. When rightly understood, these supposedly negative emotions work like indicator lights telling us we've arrived. When we don't see the path, or we're unsure about having what it takes to reach the goal, then we're closing in on a goal worth trying for.

That looks different for everyone, of course. A friend of one of my team members is a foster parent. But the journey there was far from comfortable. Lena and her husband were unprepared for their first placement, a very traumatized ten-year-old. Armed with many therapeutic theories and parenting books, Lena thought they could handle the presenting behaviors of their foster child. But the child's outbursts grew more and more intense, which was not helped by limitations to telehealth, therapy waiting lists, social distancing, virtual school, and other external factors.

After one particular crisis, the child's foster-care team decided the child could benefit from intensive medical help. This meant the child would have to move out of Lena's home. She felt like a failure. She loved her foster child deeply and felt so defeated in her desire to foster and help every child that would come into her home.

Smaller setbacks began to creep up as Lena processed her first parenting experience. She and her husband couldn't agree on when they could welcome another child into their home. They argued about small details of their home, ones never an issue before becoming parents. Lena felt fear every time she thought about having to parent another similarly aged child. She lost focus at work and isolated from friends to hide from sharing her failure.

Eventually, Lena began therapy and realized her limiting beliefs around fostering. She created liberating truths and started setting goals around parenting growth and hopeful experiences, while her therapist helped her process her traumas and the ongoing big life changes of each new foster child.

Lena and her husband have since (at the time of this writing) had eight other children walk through their front door following their first child's traumatic departure. They have had children whose ages ranged from one to seventeen. Lena now welcomes the discomfort this journey puts her in. It counters all the normal responses most of us have of wanting an easy life, let alone an easy parenting life.

"I'm driven by the desire to make a difference one child at a time, one family at a time," Lena shared. Her fear of being enough at the right time tells her she's making progress and becoming a stronger parent for children of a variety of ages. Now she leans into discomfort knowing it guides her toward new capabilities.

Most people shrink back when they feel negative emotions. Don't. They might just be markers that you're on the right path. After all, the path from the comfort zone to the discomfort zone is where growth occurs.

But how do you know if your goal is challenging or just crazy? When are the risks too great? After all, there's a difference between discomfort and delusion.

The Delusional Zone

Let's go back to GM's mistake. When GM blew its 29 percent goal and damaged its viability as a company, critics used it as a warning about the danger of goal setting. They said goal setting doesn't work, or that it causes more problems than it solves. But GM didn't fail because it set a challenging goal. It failed because it wandered into the delusional zone.

The goal encouraged tunnel vision and reckless strategies. GM was so focused on hitting 29 percent, it lost track of the rest of its business and tried hitting the goal using strategies that ultimately undercut its financial health. Relevancy, as we discussed in the SMARTER framework, can prevent this kind of self-destructive goal seeking. Some goals are simply impossible and fail to align with the rest of our priorities. They don't inspire; they ensure failure.

We can all step into the delusional zone if we're not careful. Me thinking I could play on the PGA senior tour, for instance—that's delusional. Ask anyone who's ever played golf with me. What about the guy who decided to run across four deserts? That sounds delusional, right? It does until you consider the fact that he had always been fairly athletic, was highly determined, and was running with a close-knit group of supportive fellow travelers.

What about you? How can you tell you're veering into crazy town? Sometimes it's just math. I once heard Dave Ramsey mention challenging a salesperson on his staff. The guy had set a goal of calling a certain number of leads each day. Dave told him he wasn't thinking clearly; yes, the goal was ambitious, but there simply wasn't enough time in the day to accomplish it. The salesman had lunged right over the discomfort zone into the delusional zone. He eventually scaled it back. It's easy to think of parallel cases where money or other metrics are unattainable based on bandwidth and so on. We have to believe in the possibility (Step 1), but some constraints are real.

Other times, talking with a spouse or someone close to you can help. We're rarely as good as others at identifying our blind

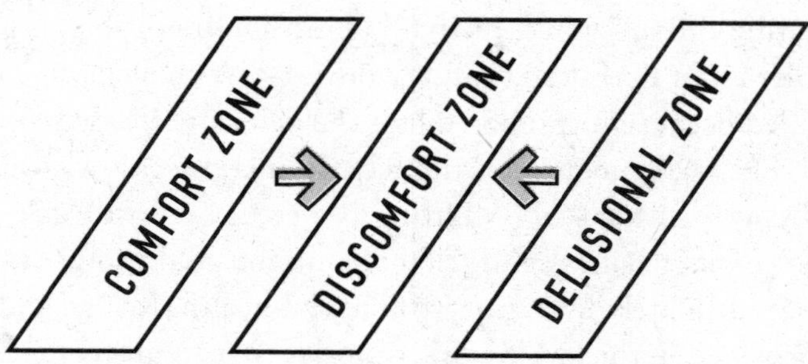

Risky goals are a must. That means discomfort is a positive indicator. When you set goals, avoid staying in your comfort zone. Be sure to avoid the delusional zone too.

spots. Other people can sometimes see how a goal is missing the relevancy we think it has.

Here's a warning. You don't need one crazy leap to land in the delusional zone. Sometimes we can drift there with the accumulated demands of multiple goals. I see this when people plan major deadlines simultaneously or stack up projects one after another without enough margin. You know what happens next. It's a train wreck just waiting to happen.

Goals in the discomfort zone challenge us and summon our best performance. Goals in the delusional zone invite defeat and merely leave us frustrated and discouraged. What I like to do is set a goal that's almost delusional and then dial it back a few clicks. Then I land somewhere in my discomfort zone.

Preparing for the Journey

I'd like to return to the story of Your Best Year Ever alum Natalee. Before moving with her family to a new city, she launched an online branding and marketing consultancy. She had started another business once before and was ready to do it again.

Natalee was able to turn a previous professional relationship into her first client, but getting traction was hard at first. "I knew I wanted to continue to grow my business, and I wanted to do something entrepreneurial," she said. But it wasn't easy with the move and young kids. Despite the challenges and uncertainty, she ventured out and set a goal to grow her business. The journey had its bumps and turns, but she figured it out along the way and took her business from one client to six. "I love that I'm being an entrepreneur," she said. "It's so liberating to do something I've always dreamed of doing. I'm very proud of the fact that I've gone out and I've done that. I've created value in the world."

Running her own business began as a dream. Then it became a daunting goal. After that, it was her day job. One year she set the goal of creating $10,000 in revenue from her business in one month. It was a stretch, and she admitted she thought it was close to the delusional zone. "I thought for sure it would take me till December," she said. But no. She actually managed it by March 30. "I literally am blown away," she said. "Limiting belief: crushed."

Natalee directly benefited from the performance boost of challenging, risky goals. And you can too. Your best year ever lives somewhere beyond your comfort zone. If that's true, and I believe it is, how can you prepare for the negative emotions that are sure to hit you during the journey? Let me suggest four ways.

First, *acknowledge the value*. We move toward what we esteem. The first step is simply to confess that getting out of your comfort zone is a good thing. This is about trading your limiting belief for a liberating truth. Say it out loud if you need to: "Getting out of my comfort zone is good for me!" Remember, unless you do so, you won't experience the growth you want, the solution you need, or the fulfillment you desire. Playing it safe is not that safe.

Second, *lean into the experience*. So many people shrink back whenever they experience pain. The problem is that this can become a habit—or worse, a way of life. Instead, embrace the discomfort. Move toward it. "What I've found is that I'm never more alive than when I'm pushing and I'm in pain, and I'm struggling for high achievement," says Karnazes. "In that struggle I think there's a magic."[13] This is an important step in accomplishing anything significant. You have to go through the realm of discomfort to get what you want in life.

Third, *notice your fear*. If you feel anxiety, trepidation, or uncertainty, that's normal. But you don't have to be controlled by it. Yes, fear can signal danger. But it can also indicate you're on your way to a breakthrough. I once met a BASE jumper in Switzerland. He told me he feels almost unbearable fear every time he jumps. He's consumed with it the moment his feet leave the mountain until his chute opens several seconds later. Why? *Maybe today's the day my chute won't open*, he thinks. Despite his fear, however, the prize is greater than the worry. When the negative emotions well up, which they invariably do, he separates himself from them, minimizes them to focus on his jump, and then goes. Often, the ability to push through fear is the only thing that separates those who succeed from those who fail.

Fourth, *don't overthink it*. This is my biggest temptation. I want to know the entire path. I want a map to the destination. Alas, I rarely get one. But that's okay. All you really need is clarity for the next step. When you get it, take the next step in faith, believing you will be given the light you need to take the next one.

Growth in the Journey

If you are out to accomplish significant things in your life, you are going to be spending a lot of time outside your comfort zone. You might as well get the most out of it. Either you can be comfortable and stagnate, or you can stretch yourself—become uncomfortable—and grow. You may think that comfort leads to happiness. It doesn't. Happiness comes from growth and feeling like you are making progress.

As we try to set risky goals, it's important to remember what goals are for in the first place. They are about getting things done, yes. But it's more than that. A goal is not just about what you accomplish. It's about what you become. Goals are about growing. A good goal causes us to grow and mature. That's because every goal is about the journey as much as—even more than—the destination. And that's exactly why setting goals outside the comfort zone is so important.

9

Achievements and Habits Work Together

I was taught that the way of progress was neither swift nor easy.

—MARIE CURIE

Don't sit down and wait for the opportunities to come. Get up and make them.

—MADAM C. J. WALKER

Suzanne is in the best shape of her life. She began running regularly in her thirties and completed her first marathon a few years later. Looking for a challenging, inspiring goal when she turned forty, she decided to run fifty marathons in fifty states by her fiftieth birthday. She calls it her "50/50×50 Challenge," and she's well on her way. Now forty-four, she's already checked twenty states off her list.

Richard retired from active Air Force duty five years ago and now teaches history at his local community college. After noticing students lacked both critical thinking and the social skills necessary for leadership, he met with his advisory board about the problem. Agreeing on the need, the board asked him to create a new leadership curriculum in time for the fall semester. Richard took a sabbatical to work on the project, finished over the summer, and started teaching the new course on schedule.

When Tom worked out a proprietary color-pairing system for his interior-decorating business, his partner Isabelle had an idea. She found a developer who helped them create a mobile app that used phone or tablet cameras to match colors and suggest options for coordinating palettes. It took several months to work out the kinks. But after input from beta users, they set a March 1 launch date. They're on track to beat it by two weeks.

Each of these hypotheticals—the 50/50×50 Challenge, the leadership curriculum, and the app launch—represents a one-time accomplishment. You'll recognize the key features. Each has a clear, definable scope and time frame for completion. We can think of these as *achievement goals*. But there's another kind of goal we also need to consider.

Bill and Nancy have an awesome marriage. It's not just that they were lucky and married the right person. It's that they have intentionally cultivated intimacy. As simple as it sounds, they have gone on a date night every week for more than two decades. This habit has provided a context in which they can have deep, meaningful conversations about the things that matter most.

Spencer is healthy and fit. Whenever he goes in for his annual physical, his doctor is amazed. He has continued to improve for each of the last five years. The surprising thing is that Spencer just turned sixty-five last year. But his health is not an accident. It all started when he began to cultivate the habit of strength training four days a week.

Claire has built a seven-figure digital business in just three years since she lost her job due to layoffs. You might be tempted to write off her success to the fact that she stumbled onto a great idea at exactly the right time. Certainly, that played a role. But if you asked her the secret to her success, she would chalk it up to her habit of making five calls every single week to close a sale, make a new connection in her industry, or pitch her business.

Unlike the first three examples, these last three don't have a defined scope or limited time frame. Instead, they represent ongoing activity. These are called *habit goals*. Both achievement and habit goals can help us design the future we want, especially if we can get the right mix and leverage their differences.

Distinctions with a Difference

As the examples above illustrate, achievement goals are focused on onetime accomplishments. They might target paying off your credit cards, hitting a financial benchmark, or finishing writing a novel. It's essential that achievement goals include deadlines.

Habit goals, on the other hand, involve regular, ongoing activity, such as a daily meditation practice, a monthly coffee date with a friend, or walking each day after lunch. There's no deadline as such because you're not trying to accomplish just one thing. You're trying to maintain a practice. Instead, there's a start date, which triggers initiation.

Look at the three corresponding achievement and habit examples in the following list for quick comparison.

Following the SMARTER framework, the achievement goals in the table are specific, measurable, and timebound, all of which drive focus and effort. When the deadline is up, we know if we've achieved the goal or not.

Both achievement and habit goals can help us design the future we want.

ACHIEVEMENT GOALS	HABIT GOALS
Run my first half-marathon by June 1.	Run 3 miles on weekdays at 7:00 p.m., starting January 15.
Increase sales revenue 20% by the close of the third quarter.	Call 4 new client prospects each week, beginning March 1.
Read 50 books this year by December 31.	Read 45 minutes each evening at 8:00 p.m., beginning immediately.

The habit goals listed also follow the SMARTER framework. That's essential for knowing what activity we are trying to maintain and the desired frequency. While habit goals do not include deadlines, they should still be timebound. The most effective habit goals have four time keys:

1. *Start date*. This is when you intend to begin installing the habit.
2. *Habit frequency*. This is how often you will observe the habit. It could be daily, specific days of the week, weekly, monthly, and so on.
3. *Time trigger*. This is when you want to do the habit. It could be a specific time each day or day of the week. It could also be tied to another regular occurrence, like "after breakfast" or "before I get in bed." It is easier to become consistent if you can do the habit at the same time each time.
4. *Streak target*. This is how many times in a row you must do the habit before you can consider it installed—that is, once the activity becomes second nature. With most habit goals, you can stop focusing on them once that happens.

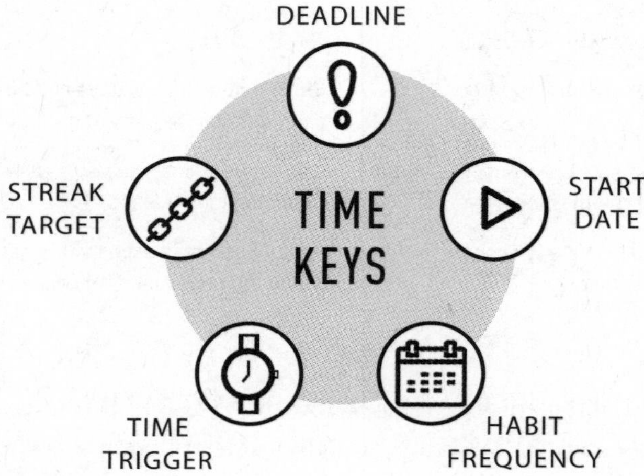

Time keys are essential for goal attainment. Deadlines work best for achievement goals. For habit goals, try combining a start date, habit frequency, time trigger, and streak target.

The risk factor comes from maintaining your streak. Installing a habit takes a period of time, and it might be longer than you think. I'll come back to this idea in Step 4.

If you're looking for help in writing effective habit goals for yourself, the sample goal templates in the back of the book have those time keys baked in. I've also included several goal detail pages from the *Full Focus Planner*, which include a Streak-Tracker™ to check off your progress.

Which Works Best?

If you're looking to create eight annual goals, you should probably have a mix of both achievement and habit goals. The trick is to know when and how to use them.

An achievement goal works for any project with a definable scope or limited time frame. Let's say you want to increase your income. You can put some definition on that and set a deadline for yourself. You could set an achievement goal like this: "Increase sales commissions by 20 percent by the end of the fiscal year." Or let's say you want to launch a new business. You can set an achievement goal like this: "Launch consultancy by June 1."

Meanwhile, a habit goal works for desires without a definable scope or limited time frame. Let's say you want to grow closer to God or become more spiritual. That's not a onetime accomplishment; that reflects an ongoing reality. You could set a habit goal like this: "Spend 20 minutes a day in Bible reading and prayer, 5 days a week at 6:00 a.m., beginning January 1, and do it for 70 days in a row." Or let's say you want to develop more intimacy with your spouse. You could set a habit goal like this: "Take my spouse out for dinner and an evening of conversation once per week, on Friday nights at 6:00 p.m., beginning March 1, and do it for 52 weeks straight."

Another way to use habit goals is as a means to complete an achievement goal. Let's say, for example, you want to write a 50,000-word book by June 30. You could identify several next steps, or you could focus on simply installing a writing habit. For example, "Write 500 words a day, 5 days a week at 6:00 a.m., beginning on February 1, and do it for 20 weeks straight."

Or maybe you want to get out of debt. This is a worthwhile achievement goal that requires strong habits. You can, for instance, set a payoff schedule (an achievement goal), but that effort will be substantially supported by some frugal habits, such as eating in rather than out or walking in your neighborhood instead of paying for the gym.

Another example: Let's say you want to increase your revenue by 30 percent before year-end. To reach that target, you'll need a strategy. Remember the example of Claire from earlier in the chapter? To reach your achievement goal, you could set the following habit goal: "Make 5 calls each week to qualified leads, beginning January 1, and do it for 52 weeks."

Different goals work for different people, and you can tailor your commitments to meet your personal emotional and physical needs. For some people, an achievement goal around health is the last thing they need. For some, it provides the motivation to get moving. For others, it's easier to settle into a healthy routine with a habit and not worry about some overarching achievement goal. That's fine. And again, some people find a mix of both types helps them get what they're after.

The great thing is that achievement and habit goals are flexible; you can structure them however you need. The main thing is to find what works for you. It might be obvious, or you might need to experiment and try out both to land on the best path.

Breaking Bad Habits

Lots of people are interested in breaking, not making, habits. And this might be you. If you have habits that might interfere with your goals, you'll likely struggle to experience your best year ever. You may, for instance,

- check your phone or social media too often
- procrastinate on important projects
- go to bed at irregular times

- complain too often about life's difficulties
- eat to manage stress or other emotions
- eat between meals
- drink more than you'd like
- binge television shows
- say yes to too many requests from others
- gossip about others when you're with friends

These and other habitual behaviors are pervasive and persistent—and they can play havoc in our lives. You may have a desire to change these behaviors, and you might even stop them for a while but then slip back into old patterns.

Habits automate our behavior. That's a plus because it saves us the trouble of consciously thinking about and deciding on our activity. We mostly just do it. But that's a double-edged sword. Once our brain automates a behavior, it can be hard to dislodge. We're overriding our programming.

Habits form when we respond to an activation trigger of some sort—could be an item, an idea, whatever—experience a reward, and then repeat the action to experience the reward again. There are a number of neurological mechanisms at play, but the basic elements are these: activation trigger, response, reward, repetition.[1]

The surest ways to break a habit are to either remove the trigger or change the response. Since the response is largely automatic, changing it can be challenging. It's doable, but sometimes people have better luck removing the trigger. Looking at our list above, for instance, we could say one way to avoid eating between meals would be to clear the pantry of snack food; to avoid checking social media, put your phone in a drawer so you can't reach for it easily; and to avoid gossiping with friends, take a break from hanging out with friends who prompt that behavior. These sorts of situational solutions work because they mute the cues to which we habitually respond. That often works better than willpower.

If you're conscious of your response, you can change it by creating rules. For instance, establish the rule that before agreeing to any new commitments, you'll always say, "Let me think about it. I'll have to check my calendar and other commitments." Or you might establish a simple rule that you'll only eat when seated for one of three meals each day; that single rule bars emotional eating and snacking. Or you might establish a rule that for every complaint you make, you have to tweet something you're grateful for. And bonus: Just creating the rule can make you more aware of your behavior. The trick is to alter your normal response—essentially to create a new and more beneficial habit.[2]

Both of these strategies are versions of precommitment, deciding in advance what you'll do about either the trigger or your probable response to the trigger. Another popular precommitment device is establishing a penalty for the habit. The "swear jar" is a classic example. Agreeing to forfeit money to a cause you dislike can work as well.

Professor Katherine Rundell, author of an acclaimed biography of John Donne, used this technique to beat procrastinating on her doctoral thesis. She agreed with a friend that if she failed to write 1,000 words each day, she'd have to donate £100 to a donkey sanctuary. "It really does work," she said. "I didn't want the donkeys to have my money. I only failed once."[3] Of course, following through on your commitment might prove difficult. I talk about the role of accountability in Step 4.

The Right Mix for You

What you're looking for is the mix of achievement goals and habit goals that's right for you. Look at your goal list. Maybe it's stacked too heavily with achievement goals. If that's the case, you might want to swap one or more with a habit goal. Maybe you have too many habit goals. Switch it up.

And don't forget the benefit of using habit goals as next steps in achievement goals. That strategy works especially well when we hit the messy middle. That's where we're headed next, after your action plan.

STEP 3

ACTION PLAN

1 Set Your Goals

Set eight goals you want to achieve for the year. Make them SMARTER:

- Specific
- Measurable
- Actionable
- Risky
- Timebound
- Exciting
- Relevant

Make sure you focus on the life domains where you need to see improvement. List just a few per quarter; that way you can concentrate your attention and keep a steady pace throughout the year.

2 Set Goals in the Discomfort Zone

The best things in life usually happen when we stretch ourselves and grow. That's definitely true for designing our best year ever. But it runs counter to our instincts, doesn't it? Follow these four steps to overcome the resistance:

1. *Acknowledge the value of getting outside your comfort zone.* It all starts with a shift in your thinking. Once you accept the value of discomfort, it's a lot easier going forward.
2. *Lean into the experience.* Most of the resistance is in our minds, but we need more than a shift in thinking. By leaning in, we're also shifting our wills.
3. *Notice your fear.* Negative emotions are sure to well up. Don't ignore them. Instead, compare the feelings to what you want to accomplish. Is the reward greater than the fear?
4. *Don't overthink it.* Analysis paralysis is real. But you don't need to see the end from the beginning or know exactly how a goal will play out. All you need is clarity on your next step. (More on this in chapter 13.)

3 Decide on the Right Mix of Achievements and Habits

Achievement goals represent onetime accomplishments. Habit goals represent new regular, ongoing activity. Both are helpful for designing your best year ever, but you need to decide on the right balance for your individual needs. The only right answer is the one that works for you.

FIND YOUR WHY

In his book *A Million Miles in a Thousand Years*, Donald Miller talks about crossing a stretch of water—not just leaving shore and arriving at the other side but also "the hard work of the middle."[1] It's a metaphor for anything meaningful we undertake. Pushing off gives us the rush of anticipation and progress. But the anticipation fades and the progress seems to slow. Pretty soon we're in the messy middle, doubting if we have the strength to make it to the other side—or maybe why we started in the first place.

In the last step, we talked about my seven-part SMARTER framework for writing powerful, effective goals. It's critical to make them specific, measurable, actionable, a little bit risky, timebound, exciting, and relevant to your actual circumstances. Now, Step 4 is about the importance of identifying and connecting with the motivations for each of your goals.

This is important because inevitably you're going to find yourself in the messy middle. It's part of every big dream, every goal, every attempt to improve. Sometimes we think if we just plan better, we can avoid the pain and breeze through to the finish. But it almost never happens that way. The answer is leveraging your motivations. It will give you the drive and stamina to finish when the going gets tough and you want to quit.

10

Your What Needs a Why

> People lose their way when they lose their *why*.
>
> —GAIL HYATT

> It all comes down to motivation. If you really want to do something, you will work hard for it.
>
> —EDMUND HILLARY

It happens to me several times a week. I want to quit. Just the other day, I wanted to quit the exercises my doctor had suggested.

I recently had surgery. There's overwhelming evidence that getting up and moving about following a surgery can decrease risks of infection, keeps blood pressure and circulation engaged, and lowers the likelihood of getting bed sores. I was up and walking around the nurses' station the morning following my surgery!

When I was leaving the hospital, I was given strict discharge instructions. I'd talked with my doctor about goals for rebuilding my strength but not overdoing it while still pushing myself toward healing. But it didn't take long for my motivation to dip once I got home.

One day in particular, I decided I didn't need my daily stretches or walk around the neighborhood. I could take a day off. I'd worked hard to this point, and I had had enough. As the day wore on, I noticed an uncomfortable and unusual tightness in my stitches and that my hands and feet were cold from lack of circulation. When I complained about my pains, my wife, Gail, pointed me back to my recovery goals. I admitted defeat, downloaded the audio of the book I was reading, and headed outdoors.

The temptation to quit is a recurring theme. If it's not my health, it is something else: my marriage, my business, my friendships, even God. This is just the nature of life. And if the voices in our heads are not enough trouble, the voices in our culture also urge us to "throw in the towel," "make a change," or "take it easy on yourself." What these same voices fail to tell you is that there is a distinction between the dream and the work required to obtain it.

"Everybody looks good at the starting line," sings Americana artist Paul Thorn. Starting is simple. It's progress that's tough. The hill is steeper than you thought. The road is longer than you assumed. You are not sure you have what it takes to finish. I have been in this spot many times. I faced it in running every half-marathon. I've seen it in my career and as an entrepreneur. I've even experienced it in my marriage and in parenting. Especially parenting.

When we begin a project, there's all kinds of enthusiasm. We're energized by that surge of excitement that comes from novelty and our own creativity. But that surge is like starter fluid; it's not the fuel that will see us through the journey. That's why so many New Year's resolutions only make it a few weeks. To go the distance with our goals, we need something stronger.

The Myth of Fun, Fast, and Easy

Everything important requires work, and sometimes there is a long arc between the dream and its realization. Some of us are more prepared to accept this than others. In her book *The Gifts of Imperfection*, Brené Brown blames our reluctance on the culture of fun, fast, and easy.[1] We are conditioned to want results now—tomorrow at the very latest. We want them without expending a lot of effort. And, of course, we must have fun doing it; otherwise, we are on to the next thing. But other than a few lucky exceptions, most payoffs are not immediate.

Unmet by the instant success we expect, we can lose heart and give up. I've seen this a hundred times in a dozen contexts:

- the spouse who is worn down after several years of marriage and is ready to walk away
- the parent who is struggling with an out-of-touch teenager and feels like giving up
- the entrepreneur who has invested months, maybe years, into a new initiative but loses heart for lack of traction
- the author who is excited about a new idea but grinds to a halt four months into writing the book
- the employee who fails to hit revenue goals and starts checking out
- the leader who is struggling to turn around a business unit and finally throws up her hands

I have personal examples galore, and I'm sure you do as well. The truth is that anything worth doing isn't all fun, it's almost never fast, and it certainly isn't easy. Remember what the IT guy said to Alia Crum? "Just another cold, dark night on the side of Everest." Whatever Everest you're climbing, you'll experience some tough points on the path, probably several.

5 Elements to Combat the Urge to Quit

When I'm tempted to quit, I stick it out by leveraging five elements. The first is *perspective*. Look at the careers of great leaders, innovators, or athletes. Was it an instant shot to the top with no setbacks for any of them? Not usually. Obstacles, reversals, and even failures are all part of their success path. That's true for everyone. We can't bank on being the exception—that's just an illusion guaranteed to derail and disappoint us even more than the problems we're facing.

Second, *a new frame*. As we discussed earlier, our expectations shape our experience. When we reframe our frustrations, we can usually find a foothold for forward momentum. Instead of letting the worst picture prevail, I ask myself empowering questions to help me push past the difficulty I face. For instance, *What could this obstacle make possible? How can I grow in this situation? What should I be learning in this challenge?*

Third, *self-compassion*. Perfectionism and self-judgment are sure to derail us. "If a thing is worth doing, it's worth doing badly," G. K. Chesterton once said. That line always makes me laugh. But it carries an essential truth: Doing imperfectly is better than not doing at all. Recall the power of liberating truths and move ahead. Give yourself a break and keep plugging away.

Doing
imperfectly
is better
than not
doing at all.

Fourth, *a sense of agency*. Don't lose sight of this. Entitlement, as Brown says, is about feeling like we deserve success. Agency is the exact opposite. It's realizing we must work to achieve it. Agency sees an obstacle and says, "I can overcome this," while entitlement complains about not being done yet. If we keep our agency, we can survive the times our dreams cease being fun, fast, or easy.

Finally, the fifth element, *your why*. This one is so important I want to spend the rest of the chapter on it. In my experience, the thing that keeps me going is answering this question: *Why am I doing this in the first place?* I then try to remember the dream. I try to get connected to the original vision, because that keeps me going when the going gets tough. No one crosses the messy middle to reach their goals unless they really want what's on the other side of discomfort. Think about parenting or getting fit or hitting a major professional goal. All of these challenges will test our perseverance. This means we have to connect with what researchers sometimes call our "autonomous motives"—reasons we find deeply, personally compelling. Why does it matter to you?

Identify Your Key Motivations

When goal pursuit is tough, it's easy to lose focus or simply want to discard the goal. If we don't stay connected to our why, as one study put it, "the infusion of goals with energy may be distressingly temporary."[2] In other words, chances are good we'll burn out and bail.

But as another study found, "Autonomous goal motives will result in greater objectively assessed persistence toward an increasingly difficult goal. . . . If individuals strive with more autonomous motives, they will be better equipped to overcome challenges in goal pursuit."[3] Your why makes all the difference in the world.

Blake is the Your Best Year Ever alum whose girlfriend dumped him two days before a giant tree landed on his house. He coped the way a lot of us do: he ate and drank his way through the stress. Coupled with letting his exercise routine go, he put on 45 pounds. He knew that had to change. As he followed the course, he assigned key motivations to each of his goals. "Once I started working my way through them, I was able to identify the importance that it had for me," he said. "Not for some exterior force or a result, but why it was important for me to achieve this. That's when I really started connecting to them and started believing that, not only were they words on a piece of paper, but this was something that, yes, I have a part in."

Blake is talking about the power of intrinsic motivations. These drivers come from our hopes, our values, our ambitions. External motivation comes from outside influences like society, our friends, our bosses, and so on. External motivations are rarely as long-lasting or effective as intrinsic motivation. "When goal pursuit is fueled by personal endorsement and valuing of the goal, commitment and persistence will be high," write the scholars of the second study quoted above. "In contrast, when goal pursuit is the outcome of pressures or external contingencies, commitment will always be 'on the line' and goal attainment will be comparatively less likely."[4] If you want to go the distance, you've got to find a reason that speaks powerfully and personally to you.

Charlie Jabaley is a great example of someone with strong intrinsic motivation. He'd achieved an extraordinary level of success in the music industry by his midtwenties, managing top artists and even winning a Grammy. He accomplished things most people could only dream of, but there was one challenge he just couldn't seem to overcome. He was wildly unhealthy and extremely overweight.

Jabaley had struggled with his weight all his life and never could quite shake his junk-food addiction. He tried dieting. He even ran three marathons, but he'd always eventually backslide into his old habits. By the age of twenty-nine, he was over 300 pounds.

But then he got diagnosed with a brain tumor. Suddenly he had a powerful new why, a stronger motivation for getting healthy: survival. He knew he had to change things. And he did. He left the successful company he had started and moved to a new city, where he overhauled his relationship with food and got help for the emotional issues fueling his eating habits. He started training for his first Ironman and lost over 120 pounds in one year. Eventually, doctors reported that his brain tumor was under control. Today, Charlie is happier and healthier than he ever was before, and he's working with a new why in mind of providing inspiration to others. Finding a powerful, personal why was what he needed to completely turn his life around.[5]

When I was running my first half-marathon, I had to get in touch with my why. It wasn't about what somebody else wanted me to do in terms of my own health. It wasn't a fundraiser somebody wanted me to run to raise money for their organization. Instead, I identified a series of motivations individually important to me. For example, I wrote this down:

1. I'm tired of being overweight.
2. I want to get into the best shape of my life.
3. I want the stamina and the energy to be able to be the most productive self I can be.

I had to identify my why. I had to see what was at stake if I achieved it. And I had to see what was at stake if I didn't achieve it. That got me through the grueling training. I needed even more for the race itself.

The truth is, I'd never run that far before. In my training, I never ran farther than nine miles. Bad idea, I know. I remember getting to mile eleven and really wanting to quit. Sometimes the messy middle waits till nearly the end. But that's what happened. I had more reasons now—and they kept me going.

I'd gone very public with my commitment to run. First and foremost, I didn't want to be embarrassed. Plus, I had convinced a ton of my colleagues to run with me. What would it look like if the CEO whose smart idea this was to begin with didn't finish it? So I said, "I've got to finish. My leadership is at stake." One thing unifies these rationales—they were all deeply personal and intrinsic.

I consider Steve Jobs a powerful example of intrinsic motivation. When he came back to Apple in the late nineties, the company was almost bankrupt. If Jobs hadn't stepped in to save the company, there would be no Apple today. No iPhone. No iPad. No iMac. No MacBook Pro. No Apple TV. No Apple Watch. These are tools I use every day of my life. But Jobs's why went deeper.

Not only did he cofound the company, he also had a radical vision for the inherent value of simple, elegant machines. That vision drove a product-line overhaul and new marketing strategy that not only saved the company but drove it to dominance. Jobs and his team got in touch with their why and changed the world.

So, what are the whys attached to your goals? One challenge in identifying your key motivations is that desire is socially mediated. Sometimes we think we want something, but the desire is actually just the reflection of what the people around us want. Our whys are copycats. Luke Burgis warns about this in his book *Wanting: The Power of Mimetic Desire in Everyday Life*. "Mimetic desire is the unwritten, unacknowledged system behind visible goals," he says, arguing that we need to focus on what he calls "thick desires" rather than "thin." We can tell the difference by asking whether our motivation is truly substantial or merely superficial.[6]

Record and Prioritize Your Key Motivations

I write key motivations as a series of bullets and usually end up with somewhere between five and seven. I recommend listing each one until you run out. After that, you'll want to prioritize them. But not all. Identify your top three. You may have plenty more, but I find it's most effective to boil your list of motivations down to just a few that really inspire you. Go through the list and rank them. Why is this important? You want to identify your most compelling motivations so you have several convincing reasons readily available to keep pressing and accomplish your goal.

For example, when Gail and I have a fight—yes, we do have fights—I ask myself, *So, why should I stay in this marriage?* Instead of pushing that question down like holding a beach ball underwater, I let it surface and embrace it. *What is at stake?* Notice, I'm not asking, *Why should I quit?* because I will get answers to that question too. The mind is tricky that way. It will attempt to answer whatever question you ask it, so be careful how you frame the question. Instead, I focus on the positive. I am looking for reasons to keep going.

Identify
your most
compelling
motivations
so you have
convincing
reasons
to keep
pressing and
accomplish
your goal.

Here's the list I keep for my marriage. When the going gets tough and the question *Why should I stay in this marriage?* arises, I have a ready resource to reorient myself:

1. Because I want love to be the defining characteristic of my life. There is no better place to learn how to love than in marriage. I really do love this woman with all my heart.
2. Because I want to be a leader, leading myself first and then my own family. Whatever else this means, it means initiative and sacrifice. That's what leaders do.
3. Because Gail is my best friend, even though we occasionally get on each other's last nerve. She is the one person I can count on to be there when I need someone to listen to me.

I have a written list like this for every important area or goal in my life. Each of the nine life domains deserves a list like this. Even for domains you may not struggle with. There may come a season when you do, and having already done this exercise will help tremendously if that season comes your way. If I get stuck and want to quit, I pull out the list and start reading through it. Immediately, it gives me perspective and energizes me. It makes it possible to silence the voices and get my head back into the race.

Over a decade ago, when I was writing my book *Platform: Get Noticed in a Noisy World*, I had a very clearly written goal: "Deliver a 50,000-word manuscript to the publisher by November 1, 2011." I had a great plan. As I started the year, I began writing. By the middle of the summer, I had a rough—very rough—draft of the manuscript that was about 50,000 words. But I had a lot of work yet to do. Then things got crazy busy toward fall. I was inundated with speaking requests, coaching inquiries, and consulting assignments. I had just launched my business, and I was reluctant to say no to anything. Well, naturally, I got buried alive. And I wasn't making any progress on the manuscript.

I could see I was going to miss the November deadline by a mile. Honestly, I got discouraged. I didn't see any way to get it done. And despite all the work I'd already invested, I wanted to give up. Then I remembered something my wife had said to me many times before: "People lose their way when they lose their *why*." That's when I remembered I had written out a bulleted list of my key motivations. I knew they would be important when the going got tough.

Here are the top three motivations I listed then:

1. I want to help tens of thousands of authors, artists, and would-be creatives who have been turned away because they don't have a platform. [This was one of my fundamental motivations for writing the book in the first place.]
2. I want to establish my authority as an expert on platform building and open the door to additional speaking engagements on this topic.
3. I want to prove that you can create a platform and use it to sell books.

When I reconnected with my key motivations—not just intellectually but emotionally—it reignited my passion. I recommitted to finishing the manuscript. I was a few weeks late, but I did it. And *Platform* went on to become a *New York Times* bestseller. All because I reconnected with my motivations. I found my why. Looking back, I find it hard to imagine what would have happened if I hadn't kept my list of key motivations for *Platform*. One thing I know for sure: my current business wouldn't exist. This book wouldn't be in your hands either.

Connect with Your Key Motivations

Now, when I say connect, I mean this in two ways. First of all, *intellectually*. It's important to have intellectual buy-in to the motivation. Maybe it's some research you've done, remarkable data, or an argument you find intellectually compelling.

Second, you need to buy in *emotionally*. Not only is it important to understand it, it's important to feel what's at stake. Anticipate what it would feel like to achieve that goal. Or, conversely, what it would feel like if you missed that goal.

One of my key motivations for strength training is to increase my energy, stamina, and productivity. I connect intellectually because I know all the research points to those outcomes. But I connect emotionally because I remember what it feels like when I'm strength training on a regular basis. Even before I exercise, I can feel that increased stamina, energy, and productivity.

When researchers at New Mexico State University tried to figure out why people like to exercise, they came back to the power of this emotional connection. Nine out of ten in one group said they exercised because they expected to feel good afterward. Seven out of ten in another group said they did it because of the sense of accomplishment they felt.[7] Writing your motivations down is important, but getting that kind of emotional connection is even more critical.

Another example comes from how I structure my week. I talk about this in my book *Free to Focus* and my Free to Focus productivity course. I divide the time in my weeks between high-leverage work, administrative work, and personal activities. I block off time to work on high-leverage work first. These are the projects that drive the most revenue for my business and intersect with my greatest passion and proficiency. Administrative work time is dedicated to the more mundane tasks of managing the business and preparing for those high-leverage activities. Personal activity time is reserved for rest and rejuvenation.

I used to work almost constantly. But then I began to see the wisdom in totally unplugging on the weekends. My key motivation is to recharge my batteries and be fully present with family and friends. I got that intellectually. The research on this point is irrefutable. That was enough to get me started. It was enough for me to commit to personal activity time. But it took a while to connect with it emotionally. I love my work, so completely disconnecting did not come naturally. Now I love the downtime and look forward to it. I'm not only intellectually committed; I'm emotionally invested as well. And that's enabled me to stay the course.

Everyone struggles to stay the course. Ray, the Your Best Year Ever alum I introduced earlier, sure did. Year after year, he made health and financial goals. Meanwhile, his health deteriorated along with his finances. Though he ran a successful business, he was spending more than he was bringing in and racked up $400,000 in consumer debt. When he told me that, I almost fell out of my chair. But that was only the start. A few years ago, Ray was diagnosed with Parkinson's, a degenerative disease that affects his central nervous system. It can be terribly debilitating.

Ray said, "I'm almost fifty years old, and I've been telling myself one day I'm going to get out of debt. One day I'm going to take care of my family. One day I'm going to build a retirement fund. One day I'm going to get in shape. One day I'm going to travel and do all the things that I promised my wife from the day we got married. And I was suddenly faced with the reality that might not come."

But as terrible as those circumstances are, Ray found his why buried inside. "I finally had that wake-up call where I realized I either had to do this now or I was never going to do it. And I also knew my family was watching. I wanted to be there for them. I want to be there for my son's wedding. I want to be there when he has my grandchildren." Those reasons, along with the desire to leave his family debt-free with a thriving business, lit a fire under him that kept him going even when he ran out of steam. "When I felt the temptation to stop or to give up, or rationalize why I shouldn't do this after all, those reasons keep me going."

When the year was over, Ray had lost more than 50 pounds. His doctor was surprised by his health. Ray also achieved a first-time-ever goal of hitting $1 million in top-line revenue for his business. And he paid off all $400,000 in consumer debt.

CONNECT WITH YOUR
KEY MOTIVATIONS

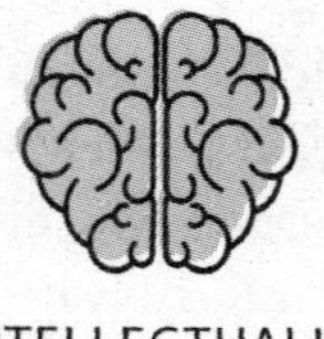

INTELLECTUALLY

EMOTIONALLY

We can know the reason why a change is good, but we won't change unless the motivation lives in both our heads and our hearts.

Another Your Best Year Ever alum, Sundi Jo, has a powerful story as well. In 2009, she entered a residential program to turn her life around. With the help of therapy and prayer, she was able to work through several traumatic experiences that had crippled her. "It was one of the hardest, most rewarding things I've ever done," she recalled. Then, in 2012, Sundi Jo felt God tell her to start a residential program for other girls in need. At first she said no. "I said no about 175,000 different times," she joked. "It was too big for me. It was too scary, and I didn't want to do it." But she felt God nudging. When tragedy struck a friend, she realized it was time.

Every year that Sundi Jo goes through the course, she adds to the vision of Esther's House of Redemption. She began with a goal to get the articles of incorporation started, then the day program, then finally the full residential program. "There are some obstacles coming up," she said, "but I remember my why." I can't tell you how excited I was when she told me she had met her goal and opened the doors of the residential program.

Bottom line: You've got to write down your motivations. And you have to connect with them, not just with your head but with your heart.

What's at Stake for You?

To get through the messy middle, when progress seems impossible, find your why. Look at your goals and ask yourself, *Why is this goal important to me personally? What's at stake both positively and negatively?* Once you've answered those questions, I recommend you list and rank your top three so you can quickly find your most compelling motivation when the going gets tough. The sample goal templates at the back have a place specifically designed to capture your key motivations.

To give you an additional edge, in the next chapter I'll share several ways you can master your motivation—even when it feels like you don't have much left.

11

You Can Master Your Own Motivation

With ordinary talent and extraordinary perseverance, all things are attainable.

—THOMAS FOWELL BUXTON

If you're not passionate enough from the start, you'll never stick it out.

—STEVE JOBS

My parents had me start piano lessons when I was five. I really didn't enjoy playing very much until about the ninth grade. Suddenly I wasn't just a piano player. I was a budding rock-and-roll keyboardist. That made all the difference in terms of my motivation.

About this same time, I took up guitar. I started with classical guitar and then, of course, began playing electric guitar. I started a band with some high school friends. I had a good feel for the instrument, but I had scales and chords to learn, songs to memorize, and a tone to mesh with other musicians.

At first we achieved a sound reminiscent of brawling alley cats. But we got better. I loved Crosby, Stills, Nash, and (sometimes) Young, so I also kept playing acoustic guitar. Then I joined the stage band when I went to college and learned to play bass.

During all of this, I experienced moments of real frustration. Sometimes I wanted to quit and find something easier. I'm glad I didn't. Not only did I develop my skills, but sticking with it taught me something essential about achievement. At first I held on to my hope of becoming a rock god. Then playing became meaningful all by itself. I still play today.

We've all seen talented, smart, and well-trained people bottom out and quit on their dreams. It takes something more to achieve our goals. Call it perseverance, persistence, or grit—it's the willingness to keep going even when the odds are bad and our enthusiasm has waned. Think of the developers of virtual reality technology, tablet computers, or ebooks. After initial spikes of interest, all of these innovations faded as failures. Yet today they are all ongoing concerns—including virtual reality—because people kept working, tinkering, and improving them. The lines of preparation and opportunity finally merged, and that can happen for us too if we stay in the game.

Next to finding your why, mastering your motivation is key for developing the necessary persistence to make it through the messy middle. I want to share four key ways to do so: finding the right reward, being realistic about the commitment, gamifying the process, and measuring your gains.

Internalize the Reward

In the last chapter, I talked about the superiority of intrinsic motivators. External motivators can work, but they're usually less effective in the long run, especially if we lose interest in the reward, get demotivated, and slack off before we're even aware. Worse, if those external rewards are someone else's idea—say, a spouse or a boss—we can become resentful of the reward if we're not careful.

Intrinsic rewards help us avoid that danger because we connect personally and emotionally with them. You might say they're self-justifying. They become an end in and of themselves, even part of our identity. I want to push that thought further by exploring how we can harness their self-perpetuating power.

Studies by Kaitlin Woolley and Ayelet Fishbach of the University of Chicago's Booth School of Business show that we tend to value an experience more when we're in the middle of doing it than when we're anticipating it on the front end or remembering it after the fact. Think about challenging activities like exercising, writing, or practicing a musical instrument. The joy comes from doing them. These findings are important because action itself can be its own reward, and the gains begin when we begin.[1]

Over time, we can train ourselves to anticipate the rewards as we internalize the benefits. If we start with a suitable intrinsic reward, such as the way our new behavior makes us feel, we will naturally begin looking forward to it. This moves the reward from mere incentive to a potent source of energy and drive.[2] I experience this with running. I feel better once I've run. When I first started running, that was enough to get me going. But having run for so long, I now look forward to that feeling. I anticipate it, and that gets me fired up before I lace up.

Mastery of an action, like my guitar playing, eventually makes it self-perpetuating. "Studies of expert performers tell us that once you have practiced for a while and can see the results," explain Florida State University psychologist Anders

Over time, we can train ourselves to anticipate the rewards as we internalize the benefits.

Ericsson and science writer Robert Pool, "the skill itself can become part of your motivation. You take pride in what you do, you get pleasure from your friends' compliments, and your sense of identity changes." The activity is fully internalized and has become its own reward. You're now a guitarist, a runner, or whatever, and maintaining the activity begins to "feel more like an investment than an expense."[3]

It's worth it, but depending on the difficulty of the goal-related activity, it might take a while.

Be Realistic about the Commitment

For as long as I can remember, I've heard it takes twenty-one days to form a new habit, thirty days at the most. If you can just marshal your willpower for three or four weeks, bingo! You've got it made. But that sure wasn't true for my running. It took far more than twenty-one days. I'm sure anyone struggling to form a new habit can identify. We all know there's got to be more to the story.

It turns out the twenty-one day "rule" is a myth with practically no scientific basis. If we're trying to do something simple and easy, it might work. But complex or challenging habits take a lot longer. Researchers at University College London tracked people attempting to form different types of new habits. Instead of three or four weeks, they found it took an average of sixty-six days for new habits to become automatic—more than three times the popular duration. And some activities, they say, would be more like 250 days![4]

It's easy to lose your why when a goal runs into overtime. It might take an additional effort to get over the hump with your habit goals. Thankfully, there are a couple of effective workarounds. For instance, we can leverage the motivation of an achievement goal to keep us going on a difficult habit goal by matching relevant achievements and habits. Running six days a week might not be your thing. But if you're emotionally connected to an achievement goal of, say, losing 20 pounds by August 1, you can leverage that motivation to help you get up early and hit the pavement. If it helps, think of habits not as ends unto themselves but as serving larger achievements. The habit essentially serves as the next step in reaching your achievement goal. It's easier to maintain the effort over time because your eye is on the bigger prize.

Chains and Games

Another trick is tracking streaks. I've included a tool to do that in the sample goal templates at the back. But this could be as simple as a check mark on your calendar. Jerry Seinfeld famously used this system to build his writing habit. The idea is to write a joke every day and mark the calendar every day you write. "After a few days you'll have a chain," he explained. "Just keep at it and the chain will grow longer every day. You'll like seeing that chain, especially when you get a few weeks under your belt. Your only job next is to not break the chain."[5]

You can use your journal or set a recurring task in your task-management system to accomplish the same thing. Our *Full Focus Planners* also have space to track these habit goals in a calendar chain. However you track the streak, the chain system can work for just about any habit.

You can set the chain to any target: miles run per day, sales calls per week, date nights with your spouse per month. Writers often use daily word count targets. The humorist Fran Lebowitz was once window shopping at Sotheby's. She was there to see furniture, but someone who knew her asked if she'd like to see an original Mark Twain manuscript. What writer wouldn't? As they looked over the pages, the man pointed out a curiosity. Twain had written little numbers in the margins. "We just don't know what those are," the man admitted. As a writer, Lebowitz did. "I happen not to be a Twain scholar, but I happen to be a scholar of little numbers written all over the place," she said. "He was counting the words."

"That's ridiculous!" the man said.

"I bet you anything," Lebowitz said. "Count." So they did—and she was right.

"Twain must've been paid by the word," the man guessed, but Lebowitz didn't think so.

"It may have nothing to do with being paid by the word," she said. "Twain might have told himself he had to write this many words each day and he would wonder, *Am I there yet?* Like a little kid in the back of a car—are we there yet?"[6] It's easy to think of works like *Tom Sawyer* and *Huckleberry Finn* in their entirety. But they too started out as big, daunting dreams that became reality one day of writing after another and keeping track along the way.

Another version of tracking is gamifying the activity. In her book, *Get It Done*, Ayelet Fishbach describes how *Pokémon Go* helped the daughter of a friend get more exercise as a diabetic. Her daily habit of walking two miles was becoming stale and boring. She stopped her streak and wasn't getting any exercise at all. Her parents and doctors would soon need to intervene with a health plan to keep her diabetes under control. After downloading *Pokémon Go* on a whim, the daughter was re-engaged with her daily walking goal—she even increased her exercise motivation because the game was so enjoyable. This story isn't unusual. Estimates peg *Pokémon Go*'s impact on extra steps taken across the US at 144 billion during the game's peak in summer 2016.[7]

A couple of years ago, I wanted to build the habit of regular hydration throughout the day. I used an iPhone app called Plant Nanny. I was entrusted with a digital plant, and every time I drank a glass of water and logged it in the app, the plant responded as if it had been watered. But if I failed to drink and log my water on schedule, the plant would get sick and eventually die. It sounds silly, but I was intent on keeping my plant alive. The game made it fun to keep a ninety-day streak going. Now the habit is internalized, and staying hydrated is its own reward. I have more energy. My thinking is better, my focus sharper. Gamifying the activity made it fun and helped me maintain the streak long enough to install the habit.

Gamifying a goal works because it heightens our intrinsic motivation to achieve. Adding an element like *Pokémon Go* or the Plant Nanny app plays to the "make it fun" strategy. And the great news is, gamifying a goal can be accomplished

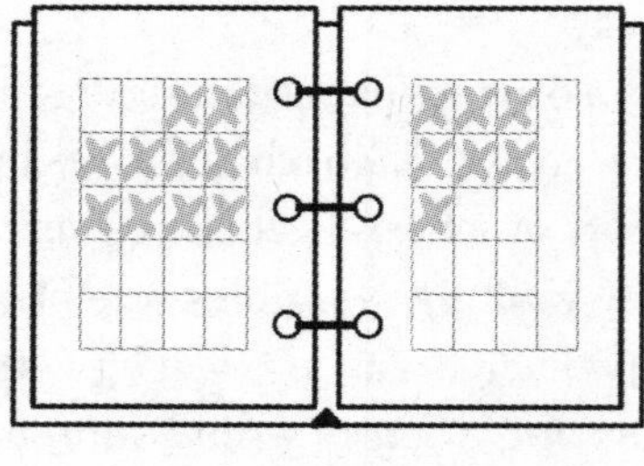

CALENDAR CHAIN

Building a habit takes time, and it's probably longer than you assume. Maintaining a calendar chain can help you sustain the effort until the habit is firmly installed.

simply by noticing the fun already around us. The daughter didn't need to invent the game to get herself up and out the door for walks. I didn't need to develop an app to pretend to keep a digital plant alive so I would drink more water. Fishbach, among many other researchers, encourages us not to reinvent the wheel when it comes to finding a way to reengage with a goal that may be going stagnant.[8]

Measure the Gain

When we set big, challenging goals, it's easy to see how far we have to go and lose enthusiasm. We can start criticizing ourselves and get dispirited. If your goal is to write a book, pay off your mortgage, build up your retirement, or whatever, it can be daunting to look up and realize how far you still have to go. That's the gap. Something I learned from Dan Sullivan has helped me rethink this problem. Dan talks about measuring the gain, not the gap.[9]

So, take a minute and look at the gain. See how far you've already come, and let your progress inspire your perseverance. This is one reason setting milestones is helpful. Not only do they help break up the big goal into manageable chunks, they give us something to measure—forward or backward. By measuring the gains, we'll not only cultivate persistence but also get a sense of our momentum.

Ayelet Fishbach offers a complementary concept she calls the "small area principle." We can feel motivated looking forward or backward during goal progress, depending on how much progress we've already made. "According to the small area principle," she says, "to sustain motivation, we need to compare our next action to whichever is smaller: the progress we've already made, or the progress we still need to make to meet the goal. At the beginning of pursuing a goal, we should look back at our completed actions. Beyond the midpoint, we should look ahead at what's still missing."[10]

If you're working, for instance, on a habit goal of 10,000 steps a day, don't dwell on the 10K as you start the day; notice instead how your count keeps climbing. You've already made 2,500 steps! But as you edge past 5,000 steps, you're better off focusing on closing the gap, especially the closer you get to your goal.

Or think of a financial goal. Let's say you're trying to bring your emergency fund up to $50,000. Early on, you'll focus on how far you've come—$5,000, $10,000, $15,000, and so on. But the closer you get to your goal, the more motivated you'll be to close the gap. Forty thousand dollars is a lot, but you won't slow down once you reach it if you've only got $10,000 to go! The initial $10,000 might have seemed big, but the final $10,000 is relatively easy by comparison—and also exciting—because of the progress you've already made.

One way to sustain our momentum is to measure the gain in real time. How? In *The 4 Disciplines of Execution*, authors Chris McChesney, Sean Covey, and Jim Huling differentiate lead and lag measures.[11] Lag measures look backward to determine whether you've met a goal. Think deadlines, finish lines, or targets. For instance, did you turn in your graduate thesis on schedule or not? Did you complete the 10K or not? Did you reach your sales goal or not? Lag measures are an excellent way to measure achievement goals because they're tied to endpoints. But they're one-offs—and they're usually a long way off. It's hard to gain a sense of momentum that way.

Lead measures work differently. Instead of looking backward, they look forward. They measure the activity that influences

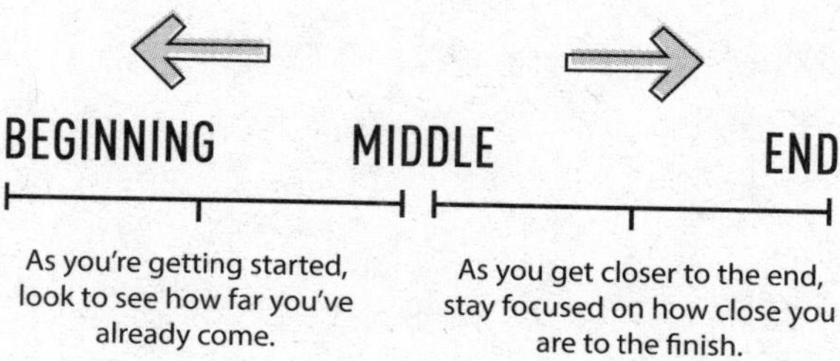

Leverage the small area principle at the beginning and end of a goal, and especially in the middle, to help you stay focused.

whether you will hit your target. For instance, if hitting your sales goal is your lag measure, then making a certain number of sales calls each week could be the lead measure. Why? Because those activities enable you to achieve your sales goal. By focusing on the right measurements, we can maintain and even accelerate our progress toward our goals.

Incremental Wins

Success is about incremental change, but we live in an instant-gratification culture where we just don't want to wait. When we take control of our motivation, however, we can stay in the game long enough to see how that incremental change adds up to major achievements. And we can do ourselves yet another favor when we pair up with our peers to achieve our goals. I'll cover that next.

12

The Journey Is Better with Friends

> Find the smartest people you can and surround yourself with them.
>
> —MARISSA MAYER

> The people with whom we interact are integral to our eventual success or failure.
>
> —BRADLEY STAATS

After the surprise success of J. R. R. Tolkien's children's novel *The Hobbit* in the fall of 1937, his publisher asked him to write a sequel. The public, he wrote, will be "clamouring to hear more from you about Hobbits!" Tolkien had no plan for a follow-up at first. "I am a little perturbed," he responded. "I cannot think of anything more to say about hobbits." The issue might have ended there, but it didn't. Tolkien mentioned that he had written more about Middle Earth, the imaginary world in which *The Hobbit* transpires. He offered to let his publisher read the material, even though it was missing the star attraction. "I should rather like an opinion, other than that of Mr. C. S. Lewis and my children, whether it has any value in itself . . . apart from hobbits."

A cog was turning in Tolkien's mind. For nearly two decades, he'd hustled at uninteresting, side writing projects to make financial ends meet. But now, despite having no real plans for a sequel, he was imagining how he might pull it off. "I must confess that your letter has aroused in me a faint hope," he continued. "I begin to wonder whether duty [the need for cash] and desire [his passion for the stories he loved] may not (perhaps) in future go more closely together."[1]

You can hear it through the tentative language: Here at last was his big chance to tell stories he loved and simultaneously improve his family's financial situation. Tolkien knew this was a life-changing opportunity. All he had to do was write another novel—preferably with more hobbits. Easy, right? It seemed so at first. By Christmas he finished the first chapter of the sequel. He was on his way! But then life happened.

Personal distractions, professional duties, and health crises seemed to pile up and prevent him from making any progress. Several times he gave up work on the project. "I have no idea what to do with it," he admitted.[2] Reading through his letters, you can spot a familiar zigzag pattern. He goes back and forth between feeling confident and close to finishing, and running out of inspiration and energy to complete the project. At one point he says his "labour of delight" has been "transformed into a nightmare."[3]

I say it's familiar because we've all experienced something similar when we've pursued significant goals. Motivation and confidence undulate like waves. So, how did Tolkien overcome the distractions and discouragement to finish *The Lord of the Rings*, one of the top-selling books of the twentieth century?

The answer starts back at the beginning with Tolkien's friend C. S. Lewis.

At several critical moments, Lewis encouraged Tolkien to stick with the project when he had given up. "Only by his support and friendship did I ever struggle to the end of the labour," Tolkien said in 1954, as the first reviews began coming in.[4] Over a decade later, he still was quick to credit Lewis for his support:

> The unpayable debt that I owe to him was . . . sheer encouragement. He was for long my only audience. Only from him did I ever get the idea that my "stuff" could be more than a private hobby. But for his interest and unceasing eagerness for more I should never have brought The *L. of the R.* to a conclusion.[5]

Tolkien had a mammoth goal, and he never would have seen it through without the help of his friend. Like it or not, we're in the same boat.

Success Is Your Social Circle

We have a very powerful myth in our culture: the myth of the self-made man or woman. But let's be honest. There's no such thing.[6] Success requires help—and usually lots of it. It's impossible to discount the influence of our social circle. That's why Solomon stresses friendships in the Proverbs. "Iron sharpens iron, and one man sharpens another," he says in one place.[7] He also warns about negative relationships: "Make no friendship with an angry man, and with a furious man do not go, lest you learn his ways and set a snare for your soul."[8]

Our peers matter. "Especially when it comes to self-improvement—like weight loss or overcoming an addiction—we need the energy of a community to stay with the program in a way

Success requires help—and usually lots of it.

that fuels us," says psychologist Henry Cloud. "Research has shown that if you are in a community that is getting healthy or overcoming something difficult, your chances of success go way up. . . . Positive energy is contagious."[9]

By being intentional on the front end, we can engineer that positive, viral energy into our best year ever. Usually we drift into peer groups. They could be associates from work, our kids' school, church, whatever. The important thing to notice is how often these relationships just happen. They're not intentional. But if iron sharpens iron, we should be careful about the kind of edge others are giving us.

Instead of random relationships, we can create communities that help everyone involved achieve their goals together—like Lewis and Tolkien.

These intentional relationships are invaluable in at least four areas. First, *learning*. Getting connected with a good group can accelerate your learning, provide key insights, help you find

Nobody has the strength to do their life alone. Let's be honest, it's a two-person job at minimum. We stand a better chance of completing our goals when we work with others.

important resources, and teach you best practices. Research shows that being with others increases our capacity to learn. When we're surrounded by new knowledge, we're more likely to "learn and act on that knowledge," according to Bradley Staats. Our information processing is also better when we're with others. Staats says, "Not only might they share information with us, but we can solve problems jointly."[10]

Encouragement. Whether it's business, family life, or our faith journey, our goals can seem impossibly tough to reach. A good peer group can give you the validation and support you need to keep going and rise above the tempests.

Accountability. We need people who can speak into our lives and help us when we're veering off track. The right peers are essential for this. We know that Edmund Hillary wouldn't have scaled Mount Everest without the help of his Sherpa guide, Tenzing Norgay. While Hillary received most of the recognition, Norgay was right beside him, keeping him going when things got tough. They never would have made it without each other.

Competition. Recall from Step 1 that abundance thinkers are not threatened by competition and even tend to value it. Why? Social pressure is a real and often beneficial force for achieving our goals. University of Pennsylvania researchers compared four groups of people who worked out over ten weeks. In one group, individuals exercised alone. In another, they exercised with social support. In a third, people exercised competitively as individuals. In a fourth, they exercised competitively as teams. The last two groups were able to compare scores with other participants, while the first two were not. The results? The two competitive groups performed *almost twice as well* as the noncompetitive groups, even when the noncompetitive group had social support.[11]

And of course it's not just about what you get. You can offer the same learning, encouragement, accountability, and competitive pressure to others in the group. That means you've got to share your goals selectively with the kind of people who can help you achieve them.

Note I said *selectively*.

Choose Your Circle Wisely

Honestly, I didn't always believe this. I used to share my goals with anyone who would listen. In fact, I even posted them on my blog for the world to see. Then I heard a TED talk from Derek Sivers, founder of CD Baby. "The repeated psychology tests have proven that telling someone your goal makes it less likely to happen," he said.[12] Why? Because your brain experiences the same sense of satisfaction as if you had actually accomplished it. It works against you. But I knew that couldn't be the whole story, could it?

I went back to the work of Gail Matthews. According to her research, people who write down their goals and share them with supportive friends do better than those who keep them private. How are we supposed to reconcile these apparently contradictory views? Like this: We share our goals, but not with everyone. Instead, we share them selectively with supportive friends. People who understand the goal-setting process. People who are willing to hold us accountable. People who are willing to call us out when we're making excuses. People who can encourage and energize us when we hit the messy middle.

The classic example of this is Alcoholics Anonymous. Charles Duhigg investigated the success of the organization for his book *The Power of Habit*. As I pointed out in Step 1, belief in the possibility of sobriety makes the difference between success and failure. But that belief is made possible by the dynamic of the support group. "At some point, people in AA look around the room and think, *If it worked for that guy, I guess it can work for me*," one researcher told Duhigg. "There's something really powerful about groups and shared experiences."[13]

Duhigg follows this line further, pointing to several examples in which being "embedded in social groups" led to personal change and transformation. One woman compared joining a group to cracking the lid on Pandora's box—in a good way. After joining the group and upgrading her outlook, there was no going back. "I could not tolerate the status quo any longer," she said. "I had changed in my core." Duhigg summarizes his findings: "Belief is easier when it occurs within a community."[14]

One of my Your Best Year Ever alumni, Scott, represents the power of our peers. After successfully reaching his goals, he said, "It's been great to be able to do this with some friends who have walked alongside me and encouraged me along the way." And the benefit was more than one-way. "I've been able to help them as well," he said. Scott and his friends put together a shared goal sheet on Google and regularly check in with each other. "My greatest piece of advice is, bring others in," he said. "That's been the most effective thing for me—to have others check on me and then others that I can hold accountable as well. It is absolutely worth it."

The right peers serve as a support structure for our liberating truths. They help us retain our belief and commitment when we hit the messy middle. The main issues are the composition of the community and the common beliefs it holds. If you surround yourself with scarcity thinkers, you'll struggle to stay motivated in the pursuit of your goals. If, on the other hand, you surround yourself with abundance thinkers, you'll gain access to encouragement, emotional and material support, solutions, insights, and more.

Ideas don't just come out of the blue. They're usually the product of conversations. When we're around the right people, we make better, more useful connections between thoughts and generate fresh and innovative approaches to our challenges. As economist Enrico Moretti says, "Being around smart people tends to make us smarter, more creative, and ultimately more productive. And the smarter the people, the stronger the effect."[15]

I started this chapter by mentioning Tolkien and Lewis. Other creative pairs demonstrate a similar dynamic. The relationship of Paul McCartney and John Lennon was sometimes competitive. Other times it was collaborative. But either way, they could not have accomplished what they did without each other.[16]

What Groups Work Best?

These peer groups can take different shapes and configurations depending on how intimate we desire them to be. Here are some examples of different groups that might work for you.

Online communities. I'm proud of the community my readers and podcast listeners have helped us build at FullFocus.co. It's a source of information and encouragement to thousands of high-achieving entrepreneurs and leaders, including me. The same is true for the private Facebook community we've created for our *Full Focus Planner*. The breakthroughs and transformations we see every week in the lives of the participants are compelling. Whatever your chosen goals, there are groups like this that can help you reach the finish line.

Running and exercise groups. You can tap into an existing community by joining an exercise class or running club. When I ran my first half-marathon, I trained by myself. But the second and third times around, I wanted the benefit of training with a group. My daughter Megan organized a team to run for a local charity. For four months leading up to the race, about thirty of us met every Saturday morning to run. Most communities have something similar. And if there isn't one in your area, why not start it yourself?

Masterminds. These peer-to-peer coaching groups are a key way to learn best practices, get feedback on challenges, and hear how others have already crossed the hurdles you're facing. These groups work best for sharing among people who are highly accomplished in their fields and who feel comfortable sharing with others. I've participated in several over the years and experienced massive gains toward my personal and professional goals.

Coaching or mentoring circles. Everyone needs a guide, preferably many. Mentors share their experience and maturity to counsel, inspire, and challenge us, whether in person or virtually. I belong to one group like this right now as a participant. And I've led several mentoring groups over the years, most recently in my business coaching program, bringing professionals together to grow through some of life's challenging and exciting moments. The trick is to realize we're all on the journey together, and some have already seen or experienced what you're going through now. The fastest way to improve and grow is to do it together, learning from those who are a bit ahead of us on the road.

Reading or study groups. There is so much to learn about life, faith, family, and business that sometimes the best way is to get a group of people around a table and study a book on the topic together. The book gives the group a track to run on, and the right chemistry among the members can create conversations that go far beyond the book itself.

Accountability groups. There are very formal accountability groups like AA or the Samson Society,[17] but they can be more informal as well, like Scott and his friends. The idea here is that members are invited to speak into each other's lives, usually around a predefined set of struggles, to encourage and challenge when needed.

Close friendships. Nothing replaces good friendships. Lewis and Tolkien's relationship went on for years, and even when it was strained, it remained beneficial to both. Without Tolkien's knowledge, Lewis even recommended *The Lord of the Rings* to the Nobel Committee for its coveted prize in literature. It didn't win, but that's the kind of belief Lewis held in his friend's work. I've found the same thing among my own friends. It's easy to place work or family ahead of these sorts of relationships, but good friendships are like supports that hold up other areas of our lives. And when a friend understands our dreams and goals, they can do more than most to support us when we struggle to stay motivated.

Don't Miss Out

Intentional relationships make us more productive, creative, and useful than we could ever be on our own. If you're like me, building these relationships can be a challenge. Professional and family demands, especially the more intimate and intensive ones, can easily interfere with building and maintaining these sorts of groups. But if you're hoping to experience your best year ever, don't miss out! They can also benefit your professional and family lives in ways so big you may never be able to measure them.

STEP 4

ACTION PLAN

1 Connect with Your Why

Start by identifying your key motivations. Why do you want to reach your goal in the first place? Why is it important personally? Get a notebook or pad of paper and list all the key motivations. But don't just list them, prioritize them. You want the best reasons at the top of your list. Finally, connect with these motivations both intellectually and emotionally.

2 Master Your Motivation

There are five key ways to stay motivated as you reach for your goals:

1. Identify your reward and begin to anticipate it. Eventually, the task itself can become its own reward this way.
2. Recognize that installing a new habit will probably take longer than a few weeks. It might even take five or six months. Set your expectations accordingly.
3. Gamify the process with a habit app or calendar chain.
4. As Dan Sullivan taught me, measure the gains. Recognize the value of incremental wins.
5. Once you're past the middle, take energy from closing the gap. You're almost there!

3 Build Your Team

It's almost always easier to reach a goal if you have friends on the journey. Intentional relationships provide four ingredients essential for success: learning, encouragement, accountability, and competition. There are at least seven kinds of intentional relationships that can help you grow and reach your goals:

- Online communities
- Running and exercise groups
- Masterminds
- Coaching and mentoring circles
- Reading and study groups
- Accountability groups
- Close friendships

If you can't find a group you need, don't wait. Start your own.

STEP 1
STEP 2
STEP 3
STEP 4
STEP 5

MAKE IT HAPPEN

At the start of the Civil War, few military careers looked as bright as General George B. McClellan's. A string of early victories not only earned him the nickname "Napoleon of the American Republic," they also catapulted him to the attention of leaders in Washington. Lincoln soon promoted him to commander of the Army of the Potomac and, later, first general-in-chief of the Union Army.

The North was excited to have McClellan at the helm. "The troops . . . under McClellan will be invincible," said the *Philadelphia Inquirer* at the news of his promotion.[1] But the enthusiasm didn't last. The new commander leapt to train his men but hesitated when it came time to attack the enemy. McClellan was constantly organizing and preparing. According to him, the army was never quite ready. All his planning and preparing meant too little action, too late to do any good.

McClellan's failure to stop General Robert E. Lee at Antietam was the direct fault of his reluctance. "Against an enemy he outnumbered better than two to one, George McClellan devoted himself to not losing rather than winning," says historian Stephen Sears. "Nor would he dare to renew the battle the next day."[2] McClellan dug in when he should have moved on. At one point, Lincoln famously wrote McClellan, "If you don't want to use the army, I should like to borrow it for a while."

Part of McClellan's problem was that he regularly overestimated the size of the enemy. The more daunting the enemy grew in his mind, the less confidence he showed in the field. Ultimately, he lost Lincoln's confidence, squandered his opportunity, prolonged the war, and cost the lives of tens of thousands of soldiers on both sides of the conflict.

McClellan demonstrates a key truth when it comes to experiencing our best year ever: Setting the goal is only half the job. The other half is taking definitive action. But how exactly do we do that? That's what we'll cover next in the final step. It's not enough to dream and plan. Realizing our goals takes action. Let's see how.

13

One Journey Is Many Steps

Dreams and reality are opposites. Action synthesizes them.

—ASSATA SHAKUR

The great doesn't happen through impulse alone, and is a succession of little things that are brought together.

—VINCENT VAN GOGH

We started this book with Mount Everest. It's a perfect metaphor for the goals we want to achieve. Another image that comes to my mind is the Empire State Building.

Stand on the sidewalk and stare up its length. It's massive. The roof towers almost a quarter mile above the ground—more than 1,200 feet—and the building tops out at just over 1,400 feet. They don't call it a skyscraper for nothing. Standing at the building's base, you can't really see the top.

Our goals can feel like that. You can imagine the end but can't see it from here. The immensity of the undertaking can sap our courage and undermine our confidence. Let's say we set an ambitious goal squarely in the discomfort zone. We can't possibly accomplish it in one go. And as we reflect on the difficulty of the undertaking, we might succumb to doubts we'll ever make it. We're not Superman, "able to leap tall buildings in a single bound." But we *can* do it in several bounds.

People regularly make it to the top of the Empire State Building all the time. In fact, you can take the stairs. There are 1,576 steps to the observation deck, and runners regularly compete to see who can get there first. If you're quick, you can do it in ten or twelve minutes. Think about that. No one can make it to the top of a skyscraper in one leap. But taking it one step at a time can get you across the finish line.

John Korff has participated in the Empire State Building Run-Up nine times. After a hip replacement a few years back and some knee trouble, the seventy-one-year-old businessman, sports promoter, and former ultramarathon runner was forced to walk his most recent trip to the top. But he did it, and when it comes to our goals, so can we if we follow the same strategy: take it one step at a time.[1] We'll look at how to get started next.

The Art of the Start

I meet people all the time who get bogged down in planning and preparation. They'd like to launch a new product, find another job, get fit, write their first book—but they just can't seem to pull the trigger. Like General McClellan, they feel unsure and unready. So they spend their time dreaming, researching, and planning. Don't get me wrong. Detailed action plans are terrific—if you're building a nuclear submarine. For most of the goals you and I will set, however, detailed planning easily becomes a fancy way to procrastinate.

At this stage of the game, the most important aspect of making it happen is practicing the art of the start. You don't have to see the end from the beginning. In fact, you *can't* if your goal is big enough. And the good news is that you don't need to. No one has to see the top of the Empire State Building from the bottom to make it all the way there. All you have to see is the next step.

Any goal is manageable one action at a time. But, like McClellan, when we let the task grow and become daunting in our minds, it can leave us feeling indecisive, discouraged, and even paralyzed with panic.

What's the alternative?

Do the Easiest Task First

Years ago, I heard a motivational speaker encourage his audience to "eat that frog." The line has a long history.[2] And it makes sense in its own way: Stop procrastinating and just do the thing you fear. Once you do that, everything else is easy. While that may be helpful in overcoming procrastination, it's exactly backward for big goals and projects. Instead, you should tackle your easiest task first.

I've written several books now, and the way I do it is almost always the same. I start with the easiest task first. I write the title page, the dedication, and the table of contents. Then I think through the chapters, pick the easiest chapter, and tackle it first. A book feels daunting. But one chapter is doable, especially if it's the easiest one. When I launch a new product, create a new program, or undertake any major goal, I operate the same way.

While we should set goals in our discomfort zone, the way to tackle a goal is to start with a task in our comfort zone. There are at least three reasons to front-load your task list with easy items, starting with *motion*. The first step on any project is usually the toughest. But when you start with the easy steps, you lower the threshold for taking action. This is how you trick your brain into starting.

Second, *emotion*. Getting some quick wins boosts your mood. According to researchers Francesca Gino and Bradley Staats, "finishing immediate, mundane tasks actually improves your ability to tackle tougher, important things. Your brain releases dopamine when you achieve goals. And since dopamine improves attention, memory, and motivation, even achieving a small goal can result in a positive feedback loop that makes you more motivated to work harder going forward."[3] That's exactly what happens for me. My excitement level goes up as I work, and it's the same for my confidence.

Third, *momentum*. Getting started and feeling good about your progress means it's easy to build momentum—just like I did with my manuscript. Gino and Staats say checking items off your list frees up mental and emotional energy to focus on other projects. You might also find that the tough items get easier as you go.

The opposite is also true. When you start with the hardest projects first, you can drain your mental and emotional energy. Now you're lagging—and still looking at a handful of small jobs on your to-do list. Suddenly the easy looks hard. It's a momentum killer. You risk getting discouraged and chucking the whole goal out the window. That's like me walking into the gym, and my trainer says let's go over to the bench press and press 150 pounds without warming up. That would be stupid.

Getting some quick wins boosts your mood.

Big goals are inherently daunting. If you're not careful, you can let them discourage you. The solution? Set your goals in your discomfort zone, but break them into a series of smaller steps in your comfort zone.

You need to warm up first. That's what identifying a next step in your comfort zone is all about.

Take the example of fitness. Let's say you set a goal to run a half-marathon this year. That goal is in your discomfort zone. You're not exactly sure how to accomplish it. Maybe you've already tried a physical challenge like that and failed. Don't let the size of the dream be its own demise. Instead of worrying how you're going to succeed, just commit to an easy next step—like calling a coach.

You're looking for one discrete task. You basically want to put the bar so low, you can fall over it. Then once that task is done, you can set the next. I don't care how big the goal is—it can be accomplished if you take it one step at a time. The sample goal templates in the back have space to break down your big goals into next steps.

What if your next step feels uncertain? Don't sweat it. Just try something and don't worry if it's wrong. The goal may be risky, but the next action isn't. That's by design. You're stepping out, but not far. If it doesn't work out, you just take another step.

Stick with the running example. Let's say you call around and can't locate a coach. Oh well. Now try posting on Facebook and seeing if any friends have a recommendation. Maybe there is a local running club you can join and train with. Whatever the situation, try something, and if you get stuck, try something else. Sometimes you have to try several different things before one works.

Seek Outside Help

Sometimes we just can't land on a next step because we're not aware of our options or we don't know what it takes to make the progress we want. The good news is, for almost every goal you want to accomplish, someone else knows how to get there—or at least has a better hunch than you. It may be a friend, an accountability partner, or a professional. You don't have to start from scratch.

A few years ago, I was really struggling with strength training. I'd been running for years, but working with weights can be tough on your own. I'd done strength training in another season of life, but this time I couldn't make any progress. I just couldn't gin up enough motivation to get started. "I'm stuck," I told a friend. "I've had this on my goal list for the last couple of years and haven't made much progress." He said, "Mike, you need to bring in an outside resource. Call a trainer." I wanted to slap my forehead because it was so obvious, but I hadn't thought of it.

I should have known better. After all, when I decided to learn photography, I found a course. When I wanted to learn to play the guitar, I hired a guitar teacher. When I decided to learn fly-fishing, I found a guide. There was no difference here. So, after the conversation with my friend, I hired a fitness trainer and started working out with him three times a week. Suddenly I got momentum and began experiencing positive results.

Outside resources are almost always helpful in finding the right next step and accelerating your achievement. And outside help can appear in a variety of guises. It doesn't have to be a professional coach. It could be a book, an article, or a podcast. It could be a friend or somebody at church. Whatever your resources, I bet you can find the help you need to get you off the dime and into motion.

If you're not sure how to move the needle in your marriage, kick-start your new business, compete in that triathlon, restore your relationship with your teenage child, save for retirement, or whatever else you've decided to do, I've got good news: Someone out there has already been to the mountain. Even if your peak is different than theirs, they can help. There's a person who knows what to do, even if you don't. Your next step could be as easy as googling to find out who.

Commit to Act

Whether you determine your next step yourself or resort to outside help, next you need to schedule it and commit to act. If it doesn't get in your *Full Focus Planner*, on your calendar, or in whatever task manager you use, it's probably not going to happen. You're never going to find time in the leftover hours of the day to accomplish your goals. You have to make time for it. You have to make it a priority and keep it like an appointment, just like you would keep with anyone else.

There's a huge difference between saying, "I'm going to try to make something happen" and "I'm going to make something happen." The first one is almost like saying, "I'm going to give it a go. If it works, great. But until I see the end result, I'm not going to fully commit."

The problem is it won't happen until you fully commit. In fact, researchers have found that when we create backup plans, we can reduce our chances of achieving our original goal. The mere existence of Plan B can undermine Plan A. How? We might divide our energies or settle for second best too soon.[4]

Scottish mountain climber W. H. Murray put it this way: "Until one is committed, there is hesitancy, the chance to draw back, always ineffectiveness. Concerning all acts of initiative and creativity, there is one elementary truth . . . that the moment one definitely commits oneself, then Providence moves too. All sorts of things occur to help one that would never otherwise have occurred. A whole stream of events issues from the decision, raising in one's favor all manner of unforeseen incidents and meetings and material assistance, which no man could have dreamt would have come his way."[5]

The Other Half of the Job

General McClellan felt certain that his goal was important. "God has placed a great work in my hands," he said when he took charge of the Army of the Potomac. "My previous life seems to have been unwittingly directed to this great end."[6] But then he stalled out. And this can happen to any one of us.

A big goal is only half the equation. If you expect to experience your best year ever, you must take action. The next two chapters will show you how. Chapter 14 shows a practical method of tracking next steps for achievement goals. And chapter 15 provides a method to take effective action on habit goals.

14

Visibility Is Essential

> It is good to repeat and review what is good twice and thrice over.
>
> —PLATO

> Planning is bringing the future into the present so you can do something about it now.
>
> —ALAN LAKEIN

General "Jimmy" Doolittle is most remembered for his daring bombing raid over Tokyo just four months after the surprise attack on Pearl Harbor, but Doolittle's most significant contribution to aviation happened many years earlier.

In 1922, he became the first pilot to fly across the US in less than twenty-four hours. He'd planned to fly by the light of the moon, but bad storms kept him in total darkness for several very dangerous hours. Luckily, he had a turn and bank indicator installed on his plane. "Although I had been flying almost five years 'by the seat of my pants' and considered that I had achieved some skill at it, this particular flight made me a firm believer in proper instrumentation for bad-weather flying,"

Doolittle said.[1] Flying with instruments was new and rare at the time, but without the indicator he might have been forced to "bail out" or just "luck it through," as other pilots were forced to do.

There had to be a better way. "Progress was being made in the design of aircraft flight and navigation instruments and radio communication. If these sciences could be merged, I thought flying in weather could be mastered," he said.[2] The right mix of instruments could give him the direction he needed in the dark. It took several years, but he figured out that a combination of radio and gyroscopes could let him fly safely regardless of visibility. And he proved it in 1929 by flying a plane with a totally blacked-out cockpit.[3]

I'd like to suggest several important parallels to achieving our goals in Doolittle's story. The first is that we often try reaching our destination without enough support. Without proper instruments, when we face bad weather—which we invariably do—we're forced to bail or just trust our luck that we'll make it. We usually don't, which is why there are all those sad statistics about New Year's resolutions. As Doolittle found, when it comes to experiencing our best year ever, we need the right mix of instruments.

This chapter provides the dashboard you need to connect your annual goals to your daily tasks. You can't just write goals and motivations. You have to *review* them to keep them top of mind as you *preview* what actions you'll take to achieve them.

Loughborough University professor Cheryl J. Travers tracked students who not only wrote down their goals but also journaled about their progress. She found that they came to greater self-awareness about their goals and their progress, including discovery of how pursuing one goal impacted their pursuit of the others. They were able to better analyze what was holding them back and what it would take to keep moving forward.[4]

Reviewing your goals and motivations will keep you ideating, self-checking, and analyzing. And that will up your resolve and stimulate creative problem-solving as you plot what to do next. I break this joint review-preview process along four separate horizons: daily, weekly, quarterly, and annual. Let's start with daily.

Daily Horizon

One of the main challenges we face with reaching our goals is losing track of them. We get distracted and sidetracked by life, and they slip out of focus. We can lose months of the year before we realize we're not making progress. A daily goal-review process can fix that problem.

It starts with a simple list of your goals, a goal summary. When I designed the *Full Focus Planner*, I placed this right up front for easy and regular viewing. But you can do this in any analog notebook, or in a digital solution like Notion, Nozbe, or Evernote. You can even frame your goals and hang them on the wall. I use a mix of analog and digital tools; you'll need to find whatever works best for you. To gain the full benefit of the daily view, you should scan this list each day. I know it sounds like a lot, but it takes only a minute—after all, you only have eight goals or so, right? I do this as part of my morning routine.

Many people feel stuck or fail to make progress because they can't make the connection between their yearly goals and their daily tasks. All their hopes languish on a wrinkled sheet of paper in a drawer somewhere. I saw this in corporate strategic planning all the time. Massive strategy documents would be created with significant goal commitments. But there was no mechanism to translate those annual and quarterly commitments to daily actions. In the end, the big binder would wind up crammed on a shelf between other big binders, rarely consulted and mostly forgotten.

The daily view is designed to make that connection between goals and tasks. As I scan the list, I look for relevant next actions. I ask myself the question, *What is it that I could do today that would move me down the field toward the goal?* That's why I call this a review-preview process. It's looking backward and forward. I'm connecting my goal list to my task list, my past commitments to my future actions.

And I don't let that list get complicated or lengthy. As I teach in my *Free to Focus* course and book, I limit my tasks to what I call my Daily Big 3. So, I never have more than three significant tasks to complete in any one day. But most of those three tasks are chosen specifically to help me achieve my goals.

A lot of people start out their day with ten or twenty tasks for the day. By close of business, they've only checked off half the items and they feel like a failure. They're creating a game they can't possibly win. Who's got time for that kind of demotivation? If you really want to make progress toward your most important goals, you need a fast and easy method to chunk down big goals into achievable daily tasks. That takes us to the weekly horizon.

Weekly Horizon

The weekly horizon goes a bit deeper and takes a bit longer, about twenty to thirty minutes. There's a triple focus of the weekly view. The first part is a mini after-action review. You'll remember the stages from Step 2, but instead of going through the process for an entire year, you just want to recap the past week. Review your progress. List your wins and your misses. Next, list the lessons you learned and what you would do differently or better. How will you adjust your behavior? Write that down too. Committing to the change on paper (or screen) will help you find clarity and build the necessary resolve.

The second part of the weekly view involves a more thorough review of your goals. Instead of scanning a list of goal statements, I want you to walk through the goal statement, your key motivations, and any relevant next steps. You want to stay intellectually and emotionally connected to your motivations. We identified those in Step 4. That wasn't an academic exercise. Ultimately the purpose of that list is to review it so you can keep your why in view. This is the secret to continuing to move forward when you want to quit.

A weekly review keeps those key motivations present in our minds. When we're in the thick of it, they can be hard to recall. But when we're reviewing our rationale week in and week out, the reasons become so internalized, we know what's at stake.

The third and final part of the weekly review is to get a sense of what needs to be accomplished for the upcoming week—a preview. As we saw with the case of General McClellan, it's critical to break down big goals into actionable next steps; otherwise, you'll fail to make the progress required to reach your goals. It's now time to turn those next steps into objectives you must accomplish in the coming week.

I call this my Weekly Big 3, and it's the best way I know to get traction and maintain momentum on those next steps. The Weekly Big 3 represents definitive outcomes I must accomplish to move closer to my goals. How does this relate to my Daily

Big 3? I use my Weekly Big 3 to dictate my Daily Big 3. Taken together, the process works like this:

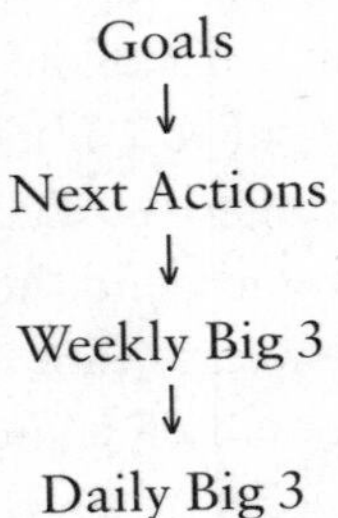

Here's an example so you can see it in action. Let's say your goal is to restore a classic Volkswagen Beetle for your daughter's sixteenth birthday, which is October 18. It's March 1. That's not a lot of time, but it's doable. And the pressure is on because you want something super special to celebrate this milestone in her life.

The most important next actions are probably purchasing a car that fits your budget and having it shipped to your house where you can begin working on it. So, how are you going to proceed? You might map out a complete project schedule, but you don't need to. The first step is buying the Bug; that much is clear. And this is where the weekly review helps you connect your goals to your daily schedule.

To move toward your goal, during your weekly review you might identify the purchase as one of your Weekly Big 3 objectives. Depending on the rest of your priorities that week, you could then schedule time to talk with your spouse about the budget on Monday, research on eBay and Autotrader on Wednesday, and purchase on Thursday. Each one of those tasks would be part of your Daily Big 3.

All the way from the goal down to the individual daily tasks, the idea is to direct your actions so you're always gaining ground.

The daily and weekly reviews make that possible. I designed my *Full Focus Planner* to offer an integrated goal-to-daily-task solution to make this process simple and straightforward. But regardless of the tools you use to implement it, the review process works like a road map to goal achievement if we're intentional.

Back to our Empire State Building analogy, each Weekly Big 3 is like a story in the skyscraper, and each Daily Big 3 is like the set of steps necessary to reach that floor. The exciting thing is this: It all adds up. Step by step, floor by floor, you can make your way all the way to the top.

Quarterly Horizon

As I mentioned in Step 3, I recommend setting goals by quarter so you space them out in the year and also to prompt action immediately instead of waiting till later in the year as a more distant deadline finally comes into view. Quarterly goal setting naturally leads to a deeper review and preview every three months. The *Full Focus Planner* has one at the end of each quarter.

I recommend doing an after-action review, same as with the weekly review-preview, only focused on the entire quarter. Beyond that, the main purpose of the quarterly review is to analyze your goals and decide if they're still relevant to your life, and then make any adjustments if not. I like to take a full day for my quarterly review. But if time is tight, I can usually do this in an hour or two.

In the quarterly view, at least five actions are possible: rejoice, recommit, revise, remove, and replace. First, you can *rejoice*. Let's say you've reached an important milestone in pursuit of one of your goals. Pause to recognize and celebrate it. I firmly believe in celebrating our wins.

You don't have to wait to achieve the entire goal. In fact, the bigger our goals, the more important it becomes to celebrate small wins along the way. The creation account in Genesis tells us God looked at everything he created and called it good. He didn't wait until the whole creation was done. He did it at each stage. That's a good model for us too.

Recognizing and rejoicing in our progress helps us stay emotionally engaged for the long haul. Celebrating triggers your brain's reward system, which, according to endurance athlete Christopher Bergland, is "a prime motivating force to help you keep pushing and achieve your goals. . . . Being self-congratulatory isn't about ego or hubris, it is about harnessing your reward circuitry and tapping your dopamine pipeline."[5] Winning helps keep us in the game. So we need to be serious about rejoicing when we score.

Second, you can *recommit* to the goal. This can be hard when you feel like giving up and walking off the field. But then you realize the game isn't over. Literally anything is possible. You never know what may happen. The only thing you can know for sure is that if you quit now, you will lose.

My daughter Marissa had a sales goal she was trying to reach but had given up before the end of the month. She thought there wasn't enough time to hit the target. I challenged her on it and asked what it would take to reach the goal. It was a bit like the story of Mura and Dorfman from Step 1. She had a limiting belief blocking her progress. But there was still time on the clock! She still had a chance to affect the outcome of the month. The moment she recognized that liberating truth, it gave her a new sense of ownership and possibility. She recommitted to the goal, marshaled her team, and beat it with only minutes to spare.

The key in this situation is to refocus on the original goal and reconnect to your why. In other words, list what is at stake.

This is why I emphasize this step when setting the goal and in the weekly preview process. What will you gain? What will you lose? Once you have these in view, you can consider new strategies or find additional resources. But you have to decide, deep in your heart, *I'm going for it*.

A regular mistake people make at this stage is getting married to their strategy. Don't conflate goals and strategies. Your goal is the what; your strategy is the how. There's nothing sacred about your strategy. You can change it at any time if it's not producing results. If we're married to our strategies and they fail us, our goals will suffer. But if we're committed to our goals, we can confidently pivot on our strategies as often as we need to hit our targets. My daughter Megan and I wrote our book *Mind Your Mindset* precisely to help with the challenge of pivoting.

If you're no longer committed to the goal, your third option is to *revise* it. This is totally valid. After all, when you are planning, you have limited knowledge. Maybe you've realized that you set the goal in the delusional zone instead of the discomfort zone. Other facts or circumstances that you could not have known about may come into play—and they may be out of your control. You do have to be careful when revising a goal. You don't want to do it just so you can stay in your comfort zone and not stretch. But you also don't need to put yourself in a no-win situation just to prove a point. Personally, I would rather recommit if I can possibly achieve a goal and revise if I can't.

When I can't recommit and I don't want to revise, the fourth option is to *remove*. Grab an eraser. Hit delete. Don't let that shock you. It's a last resort but sometimes necessary. I'm all for achieving our goals. But "the Sabbath was made for man," not the other way around. This is your game. I never met the goal police, but I'm certain they don't show up when you strike a goal off your list. If a goal is no longer relevant, if it's no longer compelling, if you've tried to revise it and you can't, remove it. If you don't, the goal will just sit there and accuse you. There's no need to pay an emotional tax like that on your own list.

If you've decided to remove a goal, I recommend you *replace* it with another you want to achieve.

What if you miss a goal? Don't obsess about it. Timing is tricky under the best of circumstances. It's doubly so with major goals. I don't always reach mine by the deadline. If you're pursuing big goals, it's normal to miss the target sometimes. The important thing is to stay in the game.

Wrapping up, I recommend looking at the five quarterly review options as a decision tree:

- **REJOICE** if you've reached your goal/milestone.
  If you're not done, then
  - **RECOMMIT** to achieve it.
    If you can't recommit, then
    - **REVISE** the goal so you can achieve it.
      If you can't revise, then
      - **REMOVE** the goal from your list.
        If you remove it, then
        - **REPLACE** it with another you want to achieve.

Annual Horizon

This view is the easiest to explain because you've already done it. Congrats! The five steps of *Your Best Year Ever* comprise the annual view: reinvigorating your sense of possibility, getting closure on the past year, setting goals for the next, identifying

Achievement is as simple as taking your goal one step at a time.

your key motivations, and executing your plan by breaking it into actionable next steps.

By maintaining visibility of your goal through quarterly, weekly, and daily reviews and previews, you are guaranteeing that your daily actions accrue to your annual goals and add up to achievement.

Why Celebrate?

Before closing this chapter, I want to come back to the subject of rejoicing. High achievers sometimes struggle with this one. I used to. After a win, I rarely stopped to celebrate before jumping into the next project. But remember the observation I quoted earlier from psychology professor Timothy Pychyl: "We experience the strongest positive emotional response when we make progress on our most difficult goals." That's only true if we stop to notice. When we achieve our goals or reach milestones along the way, we need to take the appropriate time to celebrate.

Celebrating your wins validates your work. And it's also a key component of living a full, meaningful life. After running a race in Greece called the Navarino Challenge, ultramarathoner Dean Karnazes was surprised at how the townspeople came out to celebrate the winners. They dropped their work, closed their shops, and started dancing. "These people were all willing to put aside what they were doing and join together," Karnazes says.

"If we always made decisions with our heads instead of our hearts, we'd probably live much more orderly lives," he reflects, "but they would be much less joyous. . . . How many people spend their entire lives striving for something with their nose to the grindstone, only to wake up one day and realize they haven't really lived at all?"[6]

When we skip the celebration, we cheapen our efforts. And we also shortchange our lives and the lives of those closest to us. That's why it's critical to dance across the mile markers. Bring your family into it. Bring your friends into it. But take time to celebrate. Reinforce it. Let it sink into your nervous system and power you across the goal line. To give you a leg up, I've included a reward prompt in the sample goal templates at the back so you can identify up front how you will celebrate when you accomplish your goals.

Celebrating your wins validates your work.

15

You Can Trigger Success

> The key to victory is creating the right routines.
>
> —CHARLES DUHIGG

> A solid routine fosters a well-worn groove for one's mental energies and helps stave off the tyranny of moods.
>
> —MASON CURREY

I had a habit goal I wanted to install: exercise for thirty minutes, Monday through Friday at 6:00 a.m. There was only one problem. I couldn't seem to follow through. If you've ever failed at reaching a New Year's resolution, maybe you can identify. I usually started the week well. I would exercise on Monday and again on Tuesday. But by Wednesday, I was tempted to sleep in—and often would.

Clearly something had to change if I wanted to achieve my goal. That's when I decided to focus on setting my gym clothes out the night before rather than on the goal itself. It sounds ridiculously simple, but that one practice enabled me almost effortlessly to develop the habit of regular exercise.

I later discovered I was using a version of what goal achievement researchers call *implementation intentions*. I call them activation triggers. You might remember that term from chapter 9 when I was discussing habits; that's by design. Where the review-preview process, detailed in the last chapter, is especially helpful for taking next steps in achievement goals, activation triggers leverage the mechanics of habit formation to help us gain ground with our habit goals.

These are simple statements or actions that streamline the process of reaching our goals. How? By anticipating whatever contingencies or obstacles we might face, we can cue a desired response. Instead of relying on our decision-making in the moment (when our mental and emotional resources might be at their lowest), activation triggers lock in our decisions in advance. It's another use of precommitment.

Because they address contingencies, we can think of them as simple *if-then* or *when-then* statements. They work, says social psychologist Heidi Grant Halvorson, "because contingencies are built into our neurological wiring. . . . When people decide exactly when, where, and how they will fulfill their goals, they create a

It's hard to make progress when we're stuck in behavioral ruts. Activation triggers can get us out of the ruts and remind us of new and better behaviors that will help us reach our goals.

link in their brains between a certain situation or cue ('If or when x happens') and the behavior that should follow ('then I will do y'). In this way, they establish powerful triggers for action."[1]

This sort of planning smooths out the friction we experience trying to maintain momentum and gives us a way to overcome obstacles. As researchers Thomas Webb and Paschal Sheeran point out, using an activation trigger makes us "perceptually ready" to act. "Evidence indicates that . . . responses that have been planned out in an *if-then* format are initiated more immediately, more efficiently, and with less need for conscious intent," they write.[2] According to more than two hundred studies with thousands of total participants, *if-then* planners are about three times more likely to achieve their goals than those who skip this step.[3]

So, how can you leverage that advantage for yourself? You can use activation triggers to reach your goals by following three phases.

Phase 1: Anticipate Obstacles and Determine Your Response

We must first identify the triggers that will work best for reaching the goal. In the spirit of easy next steps, make sure your activation triggers are easier to achieve than your actual goals. That's the whole point. You're warming up and creating tasks in your comfort zone so you can ultimately accomplish a goal in your discomfort zone. You're leveraging the easy to do the hard.

I have a habit goal of leaving the office promptly at 5:00 p.m. But a message or request can easily undermine my goal at the last minute. The key is to decide in advance how I will handle each of these obstacles. The *if* or *when* part of the statement is the trigger; the *then* is the response. These are like the rules we discussed in chapter 9. Here's what I came up with:

- If I get a phone call after 4:45 p.m., then I'll let it go to voice mail.
- If team members ask to talk on my way out, then I'll tell them I'm happy to talk tomorrow.
- If I have to attend a meeting at 4:00 p.m., then I'll tell the organizer I must leave the meeting by 4:55 p.m.
- When an important email arrives, I will answer it up until 4:45 p.m. and won't check email again after that point.

This kind of *if-then* planning replaces an in-the-moment decision with a predetermined cue and ideal response. "When people have formed an implementation intention, they can act [automatically], without having to deliberate on when and how they should act," say goal theorists Peter Gollwitzer and Gabriele Oettingen.[4] The heavy lifting is already done.

Phase 2: Optimize Your Activation Triggers

After you've come up with a short list of possible activation triggers, identify which ones you can optimize through elimination, automation, and delegation. Laying out my exercise clothes is one example. Here are several other activation triggers I have either used in the past or am currently using:

- Program the lights in my office to turn off automatically at 5:00 p.m. so I follow through on my goal of quitting work by 5:00 p.m.

- Ask my assistant to automatically get dinner reservations for me each Friday night at 6:00 p.m. so I follow through on my goal of a weekly date night with Gail.
- Set up focus mode on my phone, which silences notifications and pulls the apps I need for my quiet time to my home screen, so I follow through on my goal to begin the day with prayer, Bible reading, and reflection.
- Hire a fitness trainer to work with me on strength training so I follow through on my goal to do strength training Monday, Wednesday, and Friday.
- Throw out all processed food from my refrigerator and pantry so I follow through on my goal to eat only clean, whole, organic foods.
- Set up an automatic deposit to my savings account so I follow through on my goal to save a certain amount of money.
- Take my laptop out of the house so I am not tempted to get back on my computer in the evening and so I follow through on my goal to have more rejuvenation time.

Hopefully these prime the pump. Your triggers will almost certainly look very different from mine. The important thing is to identify them and build them into your life.

A major part of the activation trigger process is thinking when you're at your strongest rather than relying on your willpower when you're not. With that in mind, you can optimize your triggers to further promote success. Notice in my examples above how I have taken the trigger out of my control as much as possible using elimination, automation, and delegation. For example,

- I *eliminated* temptations that could derail me. I threw out all the processed food in my kitchen. I removed my laptop from the house.
- I *automated* my activation trigger using technology. I set up an automated phone feature to prepare for my quiet time. I programmed the lights in my office. I set up an auto-deposit to my savings account.
- I *delegated* my activation trigger to my assistant. He sets up my dinner reservations.

By taking the trigger out of your control, you're no longer relying on yourself in the moment. You're identifying contingencies and obstacle-causing temptations (such as desiring to work late or forgetting to secure a reservation) and taking care of them in advance. When the contingency arises, you've already handled it.

Take the story of Jasmine, a young millennial who recognized her addiction to social media. She procrastinated with her work and checked her phone constantly. "It's as if I'm on autopilot when I do it," she said.

Jasmine wanted to change. She wanted to limit her screen time to two hours per day. Her phone was becoming a hindrance to her job, and she wanted a promotion. She realized she couldn't just not have a phone. She enjoyed all the positive aspects of her smartphone and needed to be reachable. But she knew she couldn't depend on her own willpower in the moment to stop checking her phone when she should be working. So she went with an activation trigger, one that was not dependent on her.

She found an app that prevented her from opening social media apps during certain time periods or after hitting a screen-time limit. Jasmine set up the control app and never looked back.

At first, it was an adjustment, of course, but Jasmine has since obtained that promotion and is working toward other creative goals now that she has more time in her day.

Phase 3: Experiment Until You Nail It

This is the key to success. You're going to experience setbacks—especially if you're normal. When you hit a wall, it's time to pivot. Your goal might be sacred, but your strategy isn't. Don't give up on your goal; just change your approach.

That means modifying your activation triggers until they're working right for you. Sometimes all it takes is a small tweak. For example, when I first set a habit goal to have more rejuvenation time in the evening, I thought it would be sufficient to close my laptop but leave it in the den.

That worked for the first few days, but unfortunately, I soon started cheating by opening the lid and checking social media. I solved the problem by removing my laptop from the house. Now it remains in my office.

Whatever your goal, the trick is to simply think through the contingencies and obstacles that will prevent you from achieving it. Once you've thought through the most likely hang-ups, you can pre-respond so you know what to do the second they occur. It might take a little imagination to think through the potential obstacles to your goals, but it's worth it. Once you've used activation triggers a few times, they'll become second nature.

STEP 5

ACTION PLAN

1 Break Down Big Goals into Manageable Next Steps

Don't fall for the old "eat that frog" trap. While your goal should begin in the discomfort zone, your next step should be in the comfort zone. Do the easiest task first. If you get stumped or stuck, seek outside help. You want to build momentum early with quick wins.

2 Schedule Regular Goal Reviews

For your daily review, scan your list of goals. You want to keep your goals fresh in your mind and also think through a few specific tasks for the day that will bring you closer to achieving them. I call these my Daily Big 3.

For your weekly review, scan your goals with a special focus on your key motivations. Conduct a quick after-action review of the prior week. Preview the next actions for each of your goals and determine what three outcomes you must reach in the coming week to achieve them. I call these my Weekly Big 3, and I use them to determine my Daily Big 3.

For the quarterly review, the key is to (1) rejoice if you've completed your goal or passed a milestone, (2) recommit if you haven't, (3) revise the goal if you can't recommit to it, (4) remove the goal if you can't revise, and finally, (5) replace the goal with another you want to achieve.

3 Utilize Activation Triggers

Brainstorm the best activation triggers for you. Remember to leverage what comes easy in order to do what's hard. Don't rely on your willpower in the moment. You're going to face obstacles, so anticipate those and determine the best *if-then* response in advance. The idea is to plan your workarounds before an obstacle derails you. Then optimize your activation triggers with elimination, automation, and delegation. If you don't have it right to begin with, experiment until you nail it.

The LEAP Principle

> I learned that courage was not the absence of fear, but the triumph over it.
>
> —NELSON MANDELA

> The secret to winning isn't a secret. It's constant execution in the direction of a goal.
>
> —ALI SCHWANKE

After Gail and I had been married about two years, we bought a house together in Waco, Texas. One beautiful spring Saturday morning, not long after we moved into the new neighborhood, I heard the doorbell ring. Gail got the door.

"Honey," she called out after a moment, "I think you need to come to the front door."

I got up and walked to the front door. If you had asked me who it might be, my first guess wouldn't have been the police. But there they were, two officers in uniform.

"Are you Mr. Hyatt?" they asked.

"I am," I said.

"Sir," they said, and I could tell this wasn't going to be good, "we're here to arrest you."

"What?!" I exclaimed.

"Well," they explained, "you have a speeding ticket you failed to pay, so we're going to book you and take you downtown."

So, here I was on a Saturday morning with all my neighbors outside mowing their lawns, playing with their kids, doing all the usual weekend stuff, and a pair of police officers are walking me out to their patrol car, shoving me into the back, flipping on their lights, and driving off with me inside.

When we arrived at the station in downtown Waco, I got fingerprinted for the first time in my life and turned over all my stuff. They were about to take me back to the jail when Gail walked in with the checkbook.

"Could I just write the check for the amount?" she asked.

"Yes, you can," the officers answered. So Gail got the amount and filled out the check. As soon as she signed it and handed it over, I was off the hook. It was incredibly embarrassing—and also totally avoidable. It came down to a failure to act. I knew I had the speeding ticket. I just hadn't gotten around to paying it. I hadn't done what I knew to do. I procrastinated instead.

I can't tell you how many people do this with their goals. All those folks who set New Year's resolutions and then bail? All those people who develop lofty plans but never execute? Everyone you know who seems to wait for the next big thing to happen instead of going and making it happen? It all comes down to a failure to act.

Before we go any further, I want to recap our journey so far. We've covered a lot of ground. In Step 1, we said that to create your best year ever, you must upgrade your beliefs and embrace liberating truths about what's possible in your life. In Step 2, we discovered the power of backward thinking for completing the past, harnessing regret to reveal future opportunities, and leveraging the gratitude advantage to cultivate the abundance thinking necessary to prevail.

Then in Step 3, we saw how to design a compelling future using a mix of SMARTER achievement and habit goals and why your best year ever lies just outside your comfort zone. In Step 4, we talked about tapping into the power of intrinsic motivation, fueling your why in goal achievement, and traveling with friends to stay the course through the messy middle. Finally, in Step 5, we covered how to take action and turn those goals into reality. And guess what time it is?

If you followed the action plans for each step in this book, you've got a list of your own goals by now. Let's say you want to improve in your vocation, your marriage, and your mental health. Dreaming up big results can be emotionally satisfying and intellectually stimulating. But getting started requires action. And that can be tough. After all, how can you . . .

- make room in your schedule for date night?
- find the hours it takes to vision cast and strategically plan?
- leave the comparison trap behind and focus on the value you bring to the world?

Those are good questions. And they're important to answer. But proceeding without all the answers is not the real risk here. Not even close. The real risk is this: When facing these sorts of challenges, instead of taking action we can coast on the good feeling of the dream without taking the necessary steps to see it realized.

Earlier I quoted Arthur C. Clarke's comments about the failure of imagination (see chap. 1). We sometimes fail to achieve

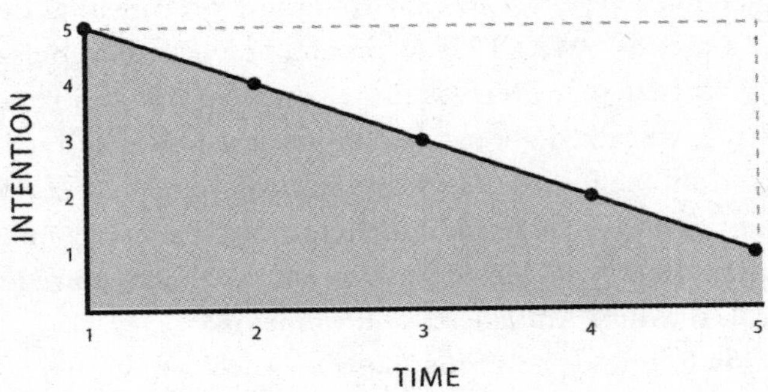

Jim Rohn noted that our intention tends to diminish the longer we wait to take action.

great goals because we can't imagine them or how we might accomplish them. They don't seem possible. But Clarke also highlights another problem, one he calls the "failure of nerve."[1]

Sometimes we can imagine exactly what we need to do. We can picture it clearly. We've defined it; we might even have a detailed plan of execution, but we don't execute. We're like General McClellan—all plans and no punch. Soon you'll be susceptible to the Law of Diminishing Intent.

It states, the longer you wait to take action, the less likely you will be to take it. Jim Rohn originally noticed this phenomenon and coined the term. But you can beat the Law of Diminishing Intent and create your best year ever by leveraging what I call the LEAP Principle:

Never leave the scene of clarity without taking decisive action.

This reminds me of another US general who had the same sense of destiny as McClellan but an outcome that was quite different. From the time he was a young man, George S. Patton imagined great things for himself as a military commander. He was born into a military family and excelled at horsemanship and other athletic endeavors, including fencing.

Like McClellan, he rocketed to stardom early in his career. He started World War I as a captain and ended as a lieutenant colonel. A pioneer in tank warfare, Patton was famous for walking in front of his brigade or even riding on top of his tanks into battle to inspire his men. "George will take a unit through hell and high water," his commander, General George C. Marshall, noted.[2]

In 1942, Marshall picked Patton to lead Operation Torch, the invasion of Axis-controlled North Africa. Patton faced all the limitations McClellan did. Right after taking the position, Patton found out his troops and supplies were insufficient. Instead of using that as an excuse for inaction, he took command and made his undersized army the most effective group of fighters he could manage. And he changed the course of history.

"It seems that my whole life has been pointed to this moment," Patton wrote just before landing in North Africa. "If I do my full duty, the rest will take care of itself."[3]

And he did. His strategy? "We shall attack and attack until we are exhausted, and then we shall attack again," he told his men.[4] That determination to act made all the difference. Patton achieved victories in North Africa and then in Sicily. After the Normandy invasion, Patton led his men six hundred miles across Europe, liberating Germany from Nazi control in 1945.

Patton took action. We need to do the same. If you want to see a big change and combat the Law of Diminishing Intent, you must be willing to take a big LEAP. It's as simple as four steps, one for each letter of the acronym:

- *Lean* into the change with expectancy. When you notice that a change is desirable or necessary, that's your green light. Punch the gas pedal. That inkling is all you need to get going.
- *Engage* with the concept until you achieve clarity. Don't let the feeling pass. Work with it until you've got a sense of what to do. That nagging thought in the back of your mind might be the start of a whole new adventure—or the ladder you need to climb out of a deep rut.
- *Activate* and do something—anything. Sometimes we wait to move until we have all the information. That's a mistake. Clarity comes in degrees. And you only need enough light for the next step. Even if you get off on the wrong foot, the rest of the journey will become clearer as you go.
- *Pounce* and do it now. Once you've determined your next step, take it. Don't wait. Waiting feels safe, but waiting kills dreams.

I've seen high achievers leverage the LEAP Principle time and again. When I hosted a mastermind group of entrepreneurs and executives called the Inner Circle, one of the members realized he needed to quit a professional organization he belonged to. The commitment was chipping away at his resources and not providing enough return.

It was a light-bulb moment, and he jumped into action. He didn't schedule it for later that week. That would have left the issue unresolved, and the delay would have allowed his intent to diminish. Why? As he built up the complications of quitting in his mind, he would have found reasons to stay on board. Instead, he left the room at the very first break, made a phone call, and resigned. He took a LEAP.

Now it's your turn. Your best year ever isn't a movie you can sit back and watch. It's a vision that needs to be built, starting now, or it won't come true. It's no accident you were drawn to this book and that you've stayed with it till the end. This is your year; this is your moment.

Don't defer your dreams. Don't delay your goals. Don't procrastinate on the one thing you need to do today to make meaningful progress in your personal or professional life. Once you've determined your next step, take it. Don't wait. Take a LEAP.

Plug-and-Play Goal Templates

Here you'll find sample goals using the templates I employ in the *Full Focus Planner*. These are all hypothetical goals that you can use to guide your goal-setting process. I've included a mix of achievement and habit goals. Your particular mix will look different; this is just to give you a sense of what's possible.

These templates demonstrate how the different elements of the Best Year Ever system fit together, including SMARTER Goals (chap. 7), key motivations (chap. 10), and next steps (chap. 13). Using templates like these makes the goal-review process (chap. 14) quick and easy.

GOAL DETAIL

☑ BODY	○ LOVE	○ MONEY
☑ MIND	☑ FAMILY	○ WORK
○ SPIRIT	○ COMMUNITY	○ HOBBIES

GOAL STATEMENT Write your SMARTER Goal.

Create a new Morning Ritual and practice it every day through June 30.

○ ACHIEVEMENT GOAL ☑ HABIT GOAL

KEY MOTIVATIONS Write, then rank, your key motivations.

3	Start each day with a win.
2	Save energy in the morning by automating my routine.
1	Have consistent time to make my kids' breakfast.

NEXT STEPS List the first few projects or tasks that make up your goal.

1	Create my new Morning Ritual.
2	Ask Beth to review and see if it works with her mornings.
3	Load my ritual into an app that automates my list each day.

CELEBRATION Decide how you'll celebrate your success.

Take a weekday off with Beth and the kids.

GOAL PROGRESS Track your achievement-goal progress.

0% 100%

STREAKTRACKER™ Track your habit-goal progress.

M1	1 ✓	2 ✓	3 ✓	4 ✓	5	6 ✓	7 ✓	8 ✓	9	10	11 ✓	12 ✓	13 ✓	14 ✓	15 ✓	16 ✓	17 ✓	18 ✓	19 ✓	20 ✓	21 ✓	22 ✓	23	24 ✓	25 ✓	26 ✓	27 ✓	28 ✓	29 ✓	30 ✓	31 ✓
M2	1 ✓	2 ✓	3	4	5	6	7	8	9	10	11	12	13	14	15	16	17	18	19	20	21	22	23	24	25	26	27	28	29	30	31
M3	1	2	3	4	5	6	7	8	9	10	11	12	13	14	15	16	17	18	19	20	21	22	23	24	25	26	27	28	29	30	31

GOAL DETAIL

- ○ BODY
- ○ MIND
- ○ SPIRIT
- ○ LOVE
- ○ FAMILY
- ○ COMMUNITY
- ☑ MONEY
- ○ WORK
- ○ HOBBIES

GOAL STATEMENT Write your SMARTER Goal.

Pay off remainder of car loan in the amount of $8,000 by August 25.

☑ ACHIEVEMENT GOAL ○ HABIT GOAL

KEY MOTIVATIONS Write, then rank, your key motivations.

2	To eliminate the stress of being in debt.
1	To have more money in our cash reserves.
3	To get rid of extra monthly payments.

NEXT STEPS List the first few projects or tasks that make up your goal.

1	Create a new monthly budget to maximize payments.
2	Determine how much extra we can put toward the car loan every month.
3	Schedule the days we will make the extra payment each month.

CELEBRATION Decide how you'll celebrate your success.

Have a celebration dinner at the fancy restaurant downtown we've been interested in.

GOAL PROGRESS Track your achievement-goal progress.

0% 100%

STREAKTRACKER™ Track your habit-goal progress.

M1	1	2	3	4	5	6	7	8	9	10	11	12	13	14	15	16	17	18	19	20	21	22	23	24	25	26	27	28	29	30	31
M2	1	2	3	4	5	6	7	8	9	10	11	12	13	14	15	16	17	18	19	20	21	22	23	24	25	26	27	28	29	30	31
M3	1	2	3	4	5	6	7	8	9	10	11	12	13	14	15	16	17	18	19	20	21	22	23	24	25	26	27	28	29	30	31

GOAL DETAIL

○ BODY
○ MIND
○ SPIRIT
○ LOVE
○ FAMILY
○ COMMUNITY
○ MONEY
☑ WORK
○ HOBBIES

GOAL STATEMENT Write your SMARTER Goal.

Write 300 words each weekday of my nonfiction book about how to manage your personal finances by November 15.

○ ACHIEVEMENT GOAL ☑ HABIT GOAL

KEY MOTIVATIONS Write, then rank, your key motivations.

2 The book will serve as a credibility builder and lead generation tool for my business.

1 A potential additional revenue stream for my business.

NEXT STEPS List the first few projects or tasks that make up your goal.

1 Schedule my writing time on my calendar for every weekday.

2 Ask two people to help me with feedback and schedule meetings in advance.

CELEBRATION Decide how you'll celebrate your success.

When the book is published, I will take my leadership team out for a nice dinner.

GOAL PROGRESS Track your achievement-goal progress.

0% — 100%

STREAKTRACKER™ Track your habit-goal progress.

M1	✓	✓	✓	✓	✓	✓	✓	✓	✓	10	✓	✓	✓	✓	✓	✓	17	18	✓	✓	✓	✓	✓	✓	✓	✓	✓	✓	29	✓	✓
M2	✓	2	✓	✓	✓	✓	7	8	✓	✓	✓	✓	✓	✓	✓	✓	✓	✓	✓	✓	21	✓	23	✓	✓	✓	✓	✓	✓	30	31
M3	1	2	3	4	5	6	7	8	9	10	11	12	13	14	15	16	17	18	19	20	21	22	23	24	25	26	27	28	29	30	31

GOAL DETAIL

○ BODY ○ MIND ○ SPIRIT ○ LOVE ○ FAMILY ○ COMMUNITY ☑ MONEY ☑ WORK ○ HOBBIES

GOAL STATEMENT Write your SMARTER Goal.

Start my side tax services business by February 7.

☑ ACHIEVEMENT GOAL ○ HABIT GOAL

KEY MOTIVATIONS Write, then rank, your key motivations.

2	Some extra income for savings and travel.
3	Hone my business skills.
1	Set a foundation for my own full-time tax services business in the future.

NEXT STEPS List the first few projects or tasks that make up your goal.

1	Build out my website.
2	Find some networking events to attend.
3	Draft shareable announcement email for current contacts.

CELEBRATION Decide how you'll celebrate your success.

After I make my first $5,000 I will go on a long weekend trip to visit my best friend.

GOAL PROGRESS Track your achievement-goal progress.

0% 100%

STREAKTRACKER™ Track your habit-goal progress.

M1	1	2	3	4	5	6	7	8	9	10	11	12	13	14	15	16	17	18	19	20	21	22	23	24	25	26	27	28	29	30	31
M2	1	2	3	4	5	6	7	8	9	10	11	12	13	14	15	16	17	18	19	20	21	22	23	24	25	26	27	28	29	30	31
M3	1	2	3	4	5	6	7	8	9	10	11	12	13	14	15	16	17	18	19	20	21	22	23	24	25	26	27	28	29	30	31

SMARTER GOAL-SETTING TEMPLATES

FOR ACHIEVEMENT GOALS

1. ________ Actionable ________ Specific, Measurable, Risky & Exciting ________ Timebound
   Relevant

2. ________ Actionable ________ Measurable, Risky & Exciting ________ Specific ________ Timebound
   Relevant

3. ________ Actionable ________ Specific ________ Measurable, Risky & Exciting ________ Timebound
   Relevant

FOR HABIT GOALS

4. ________ Actionable ________ Measurable, Risky & Exciting ________ Specific ________ Timebound
   ________ Time Trigger ________ Starting Date ________ Streak Target
   Relevant

SMARTER GOAL-SETTING TEMPLATES

FOR ACHIEVEMENT GOALS

1. Run (Actionable) the Country Music Half-Marathon (Specific, Measurable, Risky & Exciting) by April 21 (Timebound)
   Relevant

2. Read (Actionable) 50 (Measurable, Risky & Exciting) business books (Specific) by December 31 (Timebound)
   Relevant

3. Lower (Actionable) my golf handicap (Specific) from 22 to 18 (Measurable, Risky & Exciting) by September 30 (Timebound)
   Relevant

FOR HABIT GOALS

4. Walk (Actionable) two miles (Measurable, Risky & Exciting) at Pinkerton Park (Specific) M-W-F (Timebound)
   at 6:00 am (Time Trigger) starting June 1 (Starting Date) for 12 weeks (Streak Target)
   Relevant

Recommended Reading

For anyone interested in going deeper, I've listed books that can help augment each step of the methodology, along with several valuable general treatments. You can also find many worthwhile books in the endnotes.

General

Fishbach, Ayelet. *Get It Done: Surprising Lessons from the Science of Motivation*. New York: Little, Brown Spark, 2022.

Halvorsen, Heidi Grant. *Succeed: How We Can Reach Our Goals*. New York: Plume, 2012.

Locke, Edwin A., and Gary P. Latham, eds. *New Developments in Goal Setting and Task Performance*. New York: Routledge, 2013.

Milkman, Katy. *How to Change: The Science of Getting from Where You Are to Where You Want to Be*. New York: Penguin, 2021.

Napper, Paul, and Anthony Rao. *The Power of Agency: The 7 Principles to Conquer Obstacles, Make Effective Decisions, and Create a Life on Your Own Terms*. New York: St. Martin's, 2019.

Sullivan, Dan, with Benjamin Hardy. *The Gap and the Gain: The High Achievers' Guide to Happiness, Confidence, and Success*. Carlsbad, CA: Hay House, 2021.

Step 1: Believe the Possibility

Dweck, Carol S. *Mindset: The New Psychology of Success*. 2nd ed. New York: Ballantine, 2016.

Hyatt, Michael, and Megan Hyatt Miller. *Mind Your Mindset: The Science That Shows Success Starts with Your Thinking*. Grand Rapids: Baker Books, 2023.

Robson, David. *The Expectation Effect: How Your Mindset Can Change Your World*. New York: Henry Holt, 2022.

Seligman, Martin E. P. *Learned Optimism: How to Change Your Mind and Your Life*. New York: Vintage, 2006.

Sonenshein, Scott. *Stretch: Unlock the Power of Less—and Achieve More Than You Ever Imagined*. New York: Harper Business, 2017.

Step 2: Complete the Past

Pink, Daniel H. *The Power of Regret: How Looking Backward Moves Us Forward*. New York: Riverhead, 2022.

Roese, Neal. *If Only: How to Turn Regret into Opportunity*. New York: Broadway, 2005.

Smith, Jeremy Adam, Kira M. Newman, Jason Marsh, and Dacher Keltner, eds. *The Gratitude Project: How the Science of Thankfulness Can Rewire Our Brains for Resilience, Optimism, and the Greater Good*. Oakland: New Harbinger, 2020.

Step 3: Design Your Future

Burgis, Luke. *Wanting: The Power of Mimetic Desire in Everyday Life*. New York: St. Martin's, 2021.

Dean, Jeremy. *Making Habits, Breaking Habits: Why We Do Things, Why We Don't, and How to Make Any Change Stick*. Boston: Da Capo, 2013.

Easter, Michael. *The Comfort Crisis: Embrace Discomfort to Reclaim Your Wild, Happy, Healthy Self*. New York: Rodale, 2021.

Magness, Steve. *Do Hard Things: Why We Get Resilience Wrong and the Surprising Science of Real Toughness*. New York: Harper, 2022.

Wood, Wendy. *Good Habits, Bad Habits: The Science of Making Positive Changes That Stick*. New York: FSG, 2019.

Step 4: Find Your Why

Duckworth, Angela. *Grit: The Power of Passion and Perseverance.* New York: Scribner, 2016.

Grant, Heidi. *Reinforcements: How to Get People to Help You.* Boston: Harvard Business Review Press, 2018.

Hoey, J. Kelly. *Build Your Dream Network: Forging Powerful Relationships in a Hyper-Connected World.* New York: TarcherPerigree, 2017.

Step 5: Make It Happen

Hardy, Benjamin. *Willpower Doesn't Work: Discover the Hidden Keys to Success.* New York: Hachette, 2018.

Hyatt, Michael. *Free to Focus: A Total Productivity System to Achieve More by Doing Less.* Grand Rapids: Baker Books, 2019.

McChesney, Chris, Sean Covey, and Jim Huling. *The 4 Disciplines of Execution: Achieving Your Wildly Important Goals.* New York: Free Press, 2012.

Moran, Brian P., and Michael Lennington. *The 12 Week Year: Get More Done in 12 Weeks Than Others Do in 12 Months.* Hoboken, NJ: Wiley, 2013.

Oettingen, Gabriele. *Rethinking Positive Thinking: Inside the New Science of Motivation.* New York: Current, 2014.

Notes

Your Best Is Yet to Come

1. Edmund Hillary, *High Adventure: The True Story of the First Ascent of Everest* (New York: Oxford University Press, 2003), 226.

2. Tenzing Norgay, "The Great Mystery," in Peter Gillman, ed., *Everest: Eighty Years of Triumph and Tragedy* (Seattle: Mountaineers, 2000), 73.

3. Brent Yarina, "A Race to Remember," BTN, June 3, 2015, http://btn.com/2015/06/03/a-race-to-remember-i-had-no-idea-i-fell-like-that-in-inspirational-2008-run. Several videos of the race can be found online.

4. Allyssa Birth, "Americans Look to Get Their Bodies and Wallets in Shape with New Year's Resolutions," Harris Poll, January 26, 2017, https://www.prnewswire.com/news-releases/americans-look-to-get-their-bodies-and-wallets-in-shape-with-new-years-resolutions-300397268.html.

5. Laura House, "Got Ready for the Gym, Packed My Gear, Went for a Burger Instead," *Daily Mail*, January 7, 2016, http://www.dailymail.co.uk/femail/article-3388106/New-Year-s-resolutions-broken-just-one-week-2015.html.

6. Matthew Smith, "Only One in Five Making New Year's Resolutions for 2019," YouGov, December 31, 2018, https://yougov.co.uk/topics/society/articles-reports/2018/12/31/only-one-five-intend-make-new-years-resolutions-20. For full poll results, see "NYRs2019," YouGov, December 6–7, 2018, https://d25d2506sfb94s.cloudfront.net/cumulus_uploads/document/307bcd90p8/Results%20for%20Editorial%20(NYRs2019)%20293%207.12.2018.xlsx%20%20[Group].pdf.

7. Stacey Vanek Smith, "Why We Sign Up for Gym Memberships but Never Go to the Gym," NPR, January 15, 2015, http://www.npr.org/sections

/money/2014/12/30/373996649/why-we-sign-up-for-gym-memberships-but-don-t-go-to-the-gym.

8. Composite list adapted from Mona Chalabi, "How Fast You'll Abandon Your New Year's Resolutions," FiveThirtyEight, January 1, 2015, https://fivethirtyeight.com/datalab/how-fast-youll-abandon-your-new-years-resolutions/; Nichole Spector, "2017 New Year's Resolutions," NBC News, January 1, 2017, http://www.nbcnews.com/business/consumer/2017-new-year-s-resolutions-most-popular-how-stick-them-n701891; Lisa Cannon Green, "God Rivals the Gym among New Year's Resolutions," *Christianity Today*, December 29, 2015, http://www.christianitytoday.com/news/2015/december/god-rivals-gym-among-new-years-resolutions.html; "NYRs2019," YouGov; Martin Armstrong, "Top US New Year's Resolutions for 2022," Statista, January 11, 2022, https://www.statista.com/chart/26577/us-new-years-resolutions-gcs.

9. Yarina, "Race to Remember."

10. Bradley R. Staats, *Never Stop Learning: Stay Relevant, Reinvent Yourself, and Thrive* (Boston: Harvard University Press, 2018), 20.

Step 1 Believe the Possibility

1. Jan L. Souman et al., "Walking Straight into Circles," *Current Biology* 19, no. 18 (August 20, 2009): 1538–42, https://doi.org/10.1016/j.cub.2009.07.053.

Chapter 1 Your Beliefs Shape Your Reality

1. William I. Thomas and Dorothy Swaine Thomas, *The Child in America* (New York: Knopf, 1928), 572; Robert K. Merton, "The Self-Fulfilling Prophecy," *The Antioch Review* 8, no. 2 (Summer 1948); Karl Popper, *The Poverty of Historicism* (1957; repr., New York: Routledge, 2002), 11.; David Robson, *The Expectation Effect: How Your Mindset Can Change Your World* (New York: Henry Holt, 2022).

2. Chris Berdik, *Mind Over Mind: The Surprising Power of Expectations* (New York: Current, 2012), 9.

3. Quoted in Alan Shipnuck, "What Happened?," *Sports Illustrated*, April 4, 2016, http://www.golf.com/tour-and-news/what-happened-tiger-woods-it-remains-most-vexing-question-sports.

4. Carol S. Dweck, *Mindset: The New Psychology of Success* (New York: Ballantine, 2016).

5. Kelly McGonigal, *The Upside of Stress: Why Stress Is Good for You, and How to Get Good at It* (New York: Penguin Random House, 2015), 27.

6. *The Economist/YouGov Poll*, YouGov, December 12–14, 2021, p. 189, https://docs.cdn.yougov.com/pnu6yfcz0j/econTabReport.pdf.

7. Birth, "Get Their Bodies and Wallets in Shape."

8. *Economist/YouGov Poll*, 191.

9. H. A. Dorfman, *The Mental ABC's of Pitching: A Handbook for Performance Enhancement* (Lanham, MD: Rowman, 2000), 212–13.

10. Rosamund Stone Zander and Benjamin Zander, *The Art of Possibility: Transforming Professional and Personal Life* (New York: Penguin, 2002), 1.

11. "Zappos Milestone: Q&A with Nick Swinmurn," FootwearNews.com, May 4, 2009, https://footwearnews.com/2009/business/news/zappos-milestone-qa-with-nick-swinmurn-90543; "Amazon Closes Zappos Deal, Ends Up Paying $1.2 Billion," TechCrunch, November 2, 2009, https://techcrunch.com/2009/11/02/amazon-closes-zappos-deal-ends-up-paying-1-2-billion.

12. "13 Facts about Everest Expedition," Amigo Treks and Expedition, accessed February 6, 2023, https://www.amigotrekking.com/blog/everest-expedition-fact.

13. For September 2022 Berlin Marathon time, see "Marathon Results of Eliud Kipchoge," MarathonView, accessed March 21, 2023, https://marathonview.net/marathon-results-of-Eliud-Kipchoge.

14. "Kenyan Star Prepares 'Crazy' Sub-2 Marathon Bid," News24, April 4, 2017, https://www.news24.com/Sport/kenyan-star-prepares-crazy-sub-2-marathon-bid-20170403.

15. Rick Pearson, "Eliud Kipchoge: 'Breaking the two-hour marathon barrier would be like man landing on the moon,'" *Runner's World*, August 14, 2019, https://www.runnersworld.com/uk/news/a28701853/eliud-kipchoge-ineos-challenge-man-on-moon/.

16. Eric Wills, "Marathon Man," *American Scholar*, September 21, 2018, https://theamericanscholar.org/marathon-man; Sean Gregory, "'I Don't Believe in Limits.' Marathoner Eliud Kipchoge on Breaking the 2-Hour Barrier," *Time*, October 22, 2019, https://time.com/5707230/eliud-kipchoge.

17. "Real-Life 'Daedalus' Unveils Plaque to Historic Human-Powered Flight," FAI, June 11, 2016, http://www.fai.org/ciaca-slider-news/41366-real-life-daedalus-unveils-plaque-to-historic-human-powered-flight.

18. Keith Hamm, "12-Year-Old Tom Schaar Lands 1080," ESPN, March 30, 2012, http://www.espn.com/action/skateboarding/story/_/id/7755456/12-year-old-tom-schaar-lands-skateboarding-first-1080.

19. Nick Schwartz, "Watch Mitchie Brusco Become the First Skateboarder to Land a 1260," For the Win, *USA Today* Sports, August 3, 2019, https://ftw.usatoday.com/2019/08/watch-mitchie-brusco-become-the-first-skateboarder-to-land-a-1260.

20. Alex Hutchinson, *Endure: Mind, Body, and the Curiously Elastic Limits of Human Performance* (New York: William Morrow, 2018), 260.

21. Luke Burgis, *Wanting: The Power of Mimetic Desire in Everyday Life* (New York: St. Martin's, 2021), 15.

22. From a page in saxophonist Steve Lacy's notebook, published by Jason Kottke, "Advice on How to Play a Gig by Thelonious Monk," Kottke.org, February 13, 2017, http://kottke.org/17/02/advice-on-how-to-play-a-gig-by-thelonious-monk.

23. Arthur C. Clarke, *Profiles of the Future: An Inquiry into the Limits of the Possible* (New York: Harper, 1962), 14.

Chapter 2 Some Beliefs Hold You Back

1. Heidi Grant Halvorson, *9 Things Successful People Do Differently* (Boston: Harvard Business Review Press, 2012), 54–63. See also Carol S. Dweck's discussion of fixed vs. growth mindsets in her book *Mindset*, as well as her book *Self-Theories: Their Role in Motivation, Personality, and Development* (New York: Routledge, 2016). For additional insight, including populations of fixed vs. growth mindsets, see Carol S. Dweck and Daniel C. Molden, "Mindsets: Their Impact on Competence Motivation and Acquisition," in Andrew J. Elliot, Carol S. Dweck, and David S. Yeager, eds., *Handbook of Competence and Motivation: Theory and Application* (New York: Guilford, 2018), 136.

2. Dweck and Molden, "Mindsets," 136.

3. Jeremy Dean, *Making Habits, Breaking Habits: Why We Do Things, Why We Don't, and How to Make Any Change Stick* (Boston: Da Capo, 2013), 89–90.

4. Megan and I cowrote *Mind Your Mindset: The Science That Shows Success Starts with Your Thinking* (Grand Rapids: Baker Books, 2023) to help with this very problem. Part 2 of that book is all about interrogating our stories.

5. J. R. R. Tolkien, *Roverandom* (London: Harper, 2013), 110.

6. Michael Grothaus, "Here's What Happened When I Gave Up Following the News for a Week," *Fast Company*, October 25, 2016, https://www.fastcompany.com/3064824/heres-what-happened-when-i-gave-up-following-the-news-for-a-week. See also David Robson, "Catastrophising: How Toxic Thinking Leads You down Dark Paths," *BBC Worklife*, July 26, 2022, https://www.bbc.com/worklife/article/20220725-catastrophising-how-toxic-thinking-can-lead-down-dark-path.

7. Donna Freitas, *The Happiness Effect: How Social Media Is Driving a Generation to Appear Perfect at Any Cost* (New York: Oxford, 2017), 39.

8. Andrea Shea, "Facebook Envy: How the Social Network Affects Our Self Esteem," WBUR, February 20, 2013, http://legacy.wbur.org/2013/02/20/facebook-perfection.

9. Timothy D. Wilson, *Redirect: Changing the Stories We Live By* (New York: Back Bay, 2015), 52.

10. Dr. Henry Cloud, *The Power of the Other: The Startling Effect Other People Have on You, from the Boardroom to the Bedroom and Beyond—and What to Do About It* (New York: Harper, 2016), 9.

11. Christian Jarrett, *Be Who You Want: Unlocking the Science of Personality Change* (New York: Simon & Schuster, 2021), 25–52; see especially page 47, where he includes a schematic to illustrate the process.

12. Brent Schlender, *Becoming Steve Jobs: The Evolution of a Reckless Upstart into a Visionary Leader* (New York: Crown Business, 2015), 408.

13. Hillary, *High Adventure*, 7.

Chapter 3 You Can Upgrade Your Beliefs

1. Martin Luther King Jr., "Letter from Birmingham Jail," April 16, 1963, https://www.africa.upenn.edu/Articles_Gen/Letter_Birmingham.html.

2. Charles Duhigg, *The Power of Habit: Why We Do What We Do in Life and Business* (New York: Random House, 2012), 84–85.

3. Donald Miller, *Scary Close: Dropping the Act and Finding True Intimacy* (Nashville: Thomas Nelson, 2014), 12–13.

4. Erin Gruwell, *The Freedom Writers Diary: How a Teacher and 150 Teens Used Writing to Change Themselves and the World Around Them* (New York: Broadway, 2009), 49.

5. Albert Bandura, "Toward a Psychology of Human Agency," *Perspectives on Psychological Science* 1, no. 2 (June 1, 2006), https://doi.org/10.1111/j.1745-6916.2006.00011.x.

6. Martin Luther King Jr., "Living Under the Tensions of Modern Life," in *The Papers of Martin Luther King Jr.*, vol. 6, ed. Clayborne Carson and Susan Carson (Berkeley: University of California Press, 2007), 265.

7. Martin Luther King Jr., "The Quest for Peace and Justice," Nobel Lecture, December 11, 1964, https://www.nobelprize.org/prizes/peace/1964/king/lecture.

8. Julian L. Simon, *The Ultimate Resource* (Princeton: Princeton University Press, 1983).

9. Hillary, *High Adventure*, 7, 33.

10. See Peter H. Diamandis and Steven Kotler, *Abundance: The Future Is Better than You Think* (New York: Free Press, 2014) and Ronald Bailey and Marian L. Tupy, *Ten Global Trends Every Smart Person Should Know: And Many Others You Will Find Interesting* (Washington, DC: Cato Institute, 2020). See also Matt Ridley, *The Rational Optimist: How Prosperity Evolves* (New York: Harper, 2011); Hans Rowling, *Factfulness: Ten Reasons We're Wrong about the World—and Why Things Are Better Than You Think* (New York: Flatiron Books, 2018); Andrew McAfee, *More from Less: The Surprising Story of How We Learned to Prosper Using Fewer Resources—and What Happens Next* (New York: Scribner, 2019); and Marian L. Tupy and Gale L. Pooley, *Superabundance: The Story of Population Growth, Innovation, and Human Flourishing on an Infinitely Bountiful Planet* (Washington, DC: Cato Institute, 2022).

11. Vivek Wadhwa, "Why Middle-Aged Entrepreneurs Will Be Critical to the Next Trillion-Dollar Business," VentureBeat, October 31, 2014, https://venturebeat.com/2014/10/31/why-middle-aged-entrepreneurs-will-be-critical-to-the-next-trillion-dollar-business.

Step 2 Complete the Past

1. Jeremy Coon et al., *Napoleon Dynamite* (Beverly Hills, CA: 20th Century Fox Home Entertainment, 2004).

2. Dr. Benjamin Hardy, *Be Your Future Self Now: The Science of Intentional Transformation* (New York: Hay House, 2022), 22.

Chapter 4 Thinking Backward Is a Must

1. Daniel Kahneman and Dale T. Miller, "Norm Theory: Comparing Reality to Its Alternatives," in *Heuristics and Biases: The Psychology of Intuitive Judgment*, ed. Thomas Gilovich, Dale Griffin, and Daniel Kahneman (Cambridge: Cambridge University Press, 2002), 348.

2. Brené Brown, *Rising Strong: The Reckoning. The Rumble. The Revolution.* (New York: Spiegel & Grau, 2015), 270.

3. "Bob Dylan Sees Changes Blowin' in the Wind," *Mail & Guardian*, June 7, 2008, https://mg.co.za/article/2008-06-07-bob-dylan-sees-changes-blowin-in-the-wind.

4. Marilyn Darling et al., "Learning in the Thick of It," *Harvard Business Review*, July–August 2005, https://hbr.org/2005/07/learning-in-the-thick-of-it.

5. Sonja Lyubomirsky, Lorie Sousa, and Rene Dickerhoof, "The Costs and Benefits of Writing, Talking, and Thinking about Life's Triumphs and Defeats," *Journal of Personality and Social Psychology* 90, no. 4 (April 2006), https://doi.org/10.1037/0022-3514.90.4.692.

6. Carina Chocano, "Je Regrette," *Aeon*, October 16, 2013, https://aeon.co/essays/why-regret-is-essential-to-the-good-life.

7. Hardy, *Be Your Future Self*, 17–18.

8. George Santayana, *The Life of Reason* (New York: Scribner, 1905), 284.

Chapter 5 Regret Reveals Opportunity

1. Daniel H. Pink, *The Power of Regret: How Looking Backward Moves Us Forward* (New York: Riverhead, 2022), 23–24.

2. Larry Shannon-Missal, "Tattoo Takeover," Harris Poll, February 10, 2016, http://www.theharrispoll.com/health-and-life/tattoo_takeover.html.

3. The bungled tattoo examples are from the "bad tattoos" feature at TattooNow.com, originally accessed in 2017. The bored or adventurous can find a million more via Google.

4. Beatrice Aidin, "Rethinking Ink," *London Telegraph*, January 23, 2016, http://www.telegraph.co.uk/beauty/body/rethinking-ink-how-tattoos-lost-their-cool.

5. Brown, *Rising Strong*, 211.

6. Janet Landman, *Regret: The Persistence of the Possible* (Oxford: Oxford University Press, 1993), 15.

7. Brown, *Rising Strong*, 213.

8. Landman, *Regret*, 21–29.

9. Neal J. Roese and Amy Summerville, "What We Regret Most . . . and Why," *Personality and Social Psychology Bulletin* 31, no. 9 (September 2005), https://doi.org/10.1177/0146167205274693.

10. Pink, *Power of Regret*, 202–3.

11. Roese and Summerville, "What We Regret Most."

12. Sarah Graham, "Brain Region Tied to Regret Identified," *Scientific American*, August 8, 2005, https://www.scientificamerican.com/article/brain-region-tied-to-regr. See the original study here: Giorgio Coricelli et al., "Regret and Its Avoidance: A Neuroimaging Study of Choice Behavior," *Nature Neuroscience* 8 (August 2005): 1255–62, https://doi.org/10.1038/nn1514, along with follow-up here: Angela Ambrosino, Nadège Bault, and Giorgio Coricelli, "Neural Foundation for Regret-Based Decision Making," *Revue d'économie politique* 118, no. 1 (January–February 2008): 63–73, https://doi.org/10.3917/redp.181.0063.

13. Neal Roese, *If Only: How to Turn Regret into Opportunity* (New York: Broadway, 2005), 196–97.

Chapter 6 Gratitude Makes the Difference

1. Don Yaeger, "Welcome to Krzyzewskiville," *Success*, August 10, 2015, http://www.success.com/article/welcome-to-krzyzewskiville.

2. Robert A. Emmons and Anjali Mishra, "Why Gratitude Enhances Well-Being," in *Designing Positive Psychology*, ed. Kennon M. Sheldon et al. (Oxford: Oxford University Press, 2011), 254.

3. David DeSteno, Ye Li, and Jennifer S. Lerner, "Gratitude: A Tool for Reducing Economic Impatience," *Psychological Science* 25, no. 6 (April 2014): 1262–67, https://doi.org/10.1177/0956797614529979.

4. Quoted in Martha C. White, "Be Thankful, Save More," *Today*, June 13, 2014, http://www.today.com/money/be-thankful-save-more-study-says-gratitude-helps-us-reach-1D79801892.

5. Michele M. Tugade and Barbara L. Fredrickson, "Resilient Individuals Use Positive Emotions to Bounce Back from Negative Emotional Experiences," *Journal of Personality and Social Psychology* 86, no. 2 (February 2004): 320–33, https://doi.org/10.1037/0022-3514.86.2.320.

6. David DeSteno, "How Gratitude Can Help You Achieve Your Goals," in *The Gratitude Project: How the Science of Thankfulness Can Rewire Our Brains for Resilience, Optimism, and the Greater Good*, ed. Jeremy Adam Smith, Kira M. Newman, Jason Marsh, and Dacher Keltner (Oakland: New Harbinger, 2020), 53–54.

7. Emmons and Mishra, "Why Gratitude Enhances Well-Being," 250.

8. John Kralik, *365 Thank Yous: The Year a Simple Act of Daily Gratitude Changed My Life* (New York: Hachette, 2015), 14.

9. Based on interviews published in Michael Hyatt, *Set Yourself Up for Your Best Year Ever* (self-pub. PDF, 2014).

10. Based on interviews in Hyatt, *Set Yourself Up*.

11. Jeremy Adam Smith, "How to Cultivate Gratitude in Yourself," in Smith et al., *Gratitude Project*, 76–79.

12. Wilson, *Redirect*, 62–63. Incidentally, Jeremy Adam Smith recommends the same practice; see Smith, "How to Cultivate Gratitude," 75–76.

Step 3 Design Your Future

1. "Biltmore Estate's Secret Passages," *Atlas Obscura*, August 8, 2018, https://www.atlasobscura.com/places/biltmore-secret-doors-hidden-passages.

2. Robin Abcarian, "California Journal: Guns, Ghosts and Guilt: Helen Mirren Portrays the Widow Whose Winchester Mystery House Defies Logic," *Los Angeles Times*, May 10, 2017, https://www.latimes.com/local/abcarian/la-me-abcarian-winchester-mystery-20170510-story.html.

Chapter 7 Great Goals Check Seven Boxes

1. Micheline Maynard, "Incentives Still Leave GM Short of Market Goal," *New York Times*, October 22, 2002, http://www.nytimes.com/2002/10/22/business/incentives-still-leave-gm-short-of-market-goal.html.

2. Drake Bennett, "Ready, Aim . . . Fail," *Boston Globe*, March 15, 2009, http://archive.boston.com/bostonglobe/ideas/articles/2009/03/15/ready_aim_fail; Chris Woodyard, "GM Bailout Played Out over Five Years," *USA Today*, December 9, 2013, https://www.usatoday.com/story/money/cars/2013/12/09/gm-bailout-timeline/3929953.

3. See, for instance, Lisa D. Ordóñez, Maurice E. Schweitzer, Adam D. Galinsky, and Max H. Bazerman, "Goals Gone Wild," *Academy of Management Perspectives* 23, no. 1 (February 2009), http://www.hbs.edu/faculty/Publication%20Files/09-083.pdf.

4. Lawrence Tabak, "If Your Goal Is Success, Don't Consult These Gurus," *Fast Company*, December 31, 1996, https://www.fastcompany.com/27953/if-your-goal-success-dont-consult-these-gurus.

5. Gail Matthews, "The Effectiveness of Four Coaching Techniques in Enhancing Goal Achievement," presented at the Ninth Annual International Conference on Psychology, sponsored by the Athens Institute for Education and Research, May 25–28, 2015, http://www.dominican.edu/academics/ahss/undergraduate-programs/psych/faculty/assets-gail-matthews/researchsummary2.pdf.

6. Robson, *Expectation Effect*, 165. See also Cheryl J. Travers, *Reflective Goal Setting: An Applied Approach to Personal and Leadership Development* (Cham, Switzerland: Palgrave Macmillan, 2022), 33–44.

7. There are different versions of what SMART originally stood for:

Specific, Measurable, Achievable, Realistic, Timeline
Specific, Measurable, Attainable, Results-Oriented, Timely
Specific, Measurable, Attainable, Relevant, Timely

Conceptually, these are all pretty close. But, as you'll see, no one list contains all the necessary elements. Steve Kerr and Douglas LePelley, "Stretch Goals: Risks, Possibilities, and Best Practices," in *New Developments in Goal Setting and Task Performance*, ed. Edwin A. Locke and Gary P. Latham

(New York: Routledge, 2013), 23; P. J. Matre et al., "Working with Goals in Therapy," in Locke and Latham, *New Developments*, 479; Charles Duhigg, *Smarter Faster Better* (New York: Random House, 2016), 116.

8. Johnmarshall Reeve, *Understanding Motivation and Emotion*, 7th ed. (Hoboken, NJ: Wiley, 2018), 188.

9. Edwin A. Locke and Gary P. Latham, "Goal Setting Theory," in Locke and Latham, *New Developments*, 5.

10. Gabriele Oettingen, Karoline Schnetter, and Hyeon Ju Pak, "Self-Regulation of Goal Setting: Turning Free Fantasies about the Future into Binding Goals," *Journal of Personality and Social Psychology* 80, no. 5 (May 2001): 736–53, https://doi.org/10.1037/0022-3514.80.5.736.

11. Scott G. Wallace and Jordan Etkin, "How Goal Specificity Shapes Motivation: A Reference Points Perspective," *Journal of Consumer Research* 44, no. 5 (February 2018): 1033–51, https://doi.org/10.1093/jcr/ucx082.

12. Timothy A. Pychyl, "Goal Progress and Happiness," *Psychology Today*, June 7, 2008, https://www.psychologytoday.com/blog/dont-delay/200806/goal-progress-and-happiness.

13. Charles S. Carver and Michael F. Scheier, *On the Self-Regulation of Behavior* (Cambridge: Cambridge University Press, 1998), 123.

14. Reeve, *Understanding Motivation and Emotion*, 190.

15. John Doerr, *Measure What Matters: How Google, Bono, and the Gates Foundation Rock the World with OKRs* (New York: Penguin Random House, 2018), 234–44.

16. Locke and Latham, "Goal Setting Theory," 5.

17. Daniel Kahneman, *Thinking, Fast and Slow* (New York: FSG, 2011), 302–3.

18. Heidi Grant, "Here's What Really Happens When You Extend a Deadline," *Harvard Business Review*, August 19, 2013, https://hbr.org/2013/08/heres-what-really-happens-when.

19. Locke and Latham, "Goal Setting Theory," 9.

20. Sarah Milne, Sheina Orbell, and Paschal Sheeran, "Combining Motivational and Volitional Interventions to Promote Exercise Participation," *British Journal of Health Psychology* 7, no. 2 (2002): 163–84, https://doi.org/10.1348/135910702169420.

21. Alice G. Walton, "What Happened to Your Goals?," *Chicago Booth Review*, February 23, 2017, http://review.chicagobooth.edu/behavioral-science/2017/article/what-happened-your-goals.

22. Mike Gayle, *The To-Do List* (London: Hodder & Stoughton, 2009).

Chapter 8 Seriously, Risk Is Your Friend

1. Dean Karnazes, *The Road to Sparta: Reliving the Ancient Battle and Epic Run That Inspired the World's Greatest Footrace* (New York: Rodale, 2016).

2. Katie Arnold, "Drafting Dean: Interview Outtakes," *Outside*, December 8, 2006, https://www.outsideonline.com/1885421/drafting-dean-interview-outtakes.

3. See D. Christopher Kayes, *Destructive Goal Pursuit: The Mount Everest Disaster* (New York: Palgrave, 2006), along with Ordóñez et al., "Goals Gone Wild."

4. "The Quantified Serf," *The Economist*, March 5, 2015, https://medium.com/s/creative-destruction/the-quantified-serf-413ad8619a99.

5. Charles Moore, *Daniel H. Burnham: Architect, Planner of Cities* (Boston: Houghton Mifflin, 1921), 147.

6. *Desert Runners*, directed by Jennifer Steinman (Oakland, CA: Smush Media, 2013).

7. Roy M. Wallack, "Why Magician Penn Jillette Fasts 23 Hours a Day to Maintain His 100-Pound Weight Loss," *Los Angeles Times*, June 15, 2019, https://www.latimes.com/health/la-he-penn-jillette-weight-loss-20190615-story.html.

8. Katherine Mangu-Ward, "Interview: Penn Jillette," *Reason*, January 2017, https://reason.com/2016/12/21/penn-jillette.

9. Kerr and LePelley, "Stretch Goals," 21.

10. McGonigal, *Upside of Stress*, 86.

11. Kerr and LePelley, "Stretch Goals," 23–24.

12. Kerr and LePelley, "Stretch Goals," 29.

13. Quoted in Arnold, "Drafting Dean."

Chapter 9 Achievements and Habits Work Together

1. See Wendy Wood, *Good Habits, Bad Habits: The Science of Making Positive Changes That Stick* (New York: FSG, 2019), 83–144; Russell A. Poldrack, *Hard to Break: Why Our Brains Make Habits Stick* (Princeton: Princeton University Press, 2021), 45–59; Duhigg, *Power of Habit*, 31–59; and Dean, *Making Habits*, 131–70.

2. Poldrack, *Hard to Break*, 165–66.

3. "Katherine Rundell on the Art of Words (Ep. 168)," interview by Tyler Cowen, *Conversations with Tyler* podcast, January 11, 2023, https://conversationswithtyler.com/episodes/katherine-rundell.

Step 4 Find Your Why

1. Donald Miller, *A Million Miles in a Thousand Years: What I Learned While Editing My Life* (Nashville: Thomas Nelson, 2009), 177–79.

Chapter 10 Your What Needs a Why

1. Brené Brown, *The Gifts of Imperfection: Let Go of Who You Think You're Supposed to Be and Embrace Who You Are* (Center City, MN: Hazelden, 2010), 66.

2. Kennon M. Sheldon and Andrew J. Elliot, "Goal Striving, Need Satisfaction, and Longitudinal Well-Being," *Journal of Personality and Social Psychology* 76, no. 3 (1999), https://selfdeterminationtheory.org/SDT/documents/1999_SheldonElliot.pdf.

3. Nikos Ntoumanis et al., "When the Going Gets Tough: The 'Why' of Goal Striving Matters," *Journal of Personality* 82, no. 3 (June 2014): 225–36, https://doi.org/10.1111/jopy.12047.

4. Ntoumanis et al., "Going Gets Tough."

5. Aisha Nga, "Hip-Hop Mogul Leaves His Business Behind to Focus on Health," CNN, July 30, 2018, https://www.cnn.com/2018/07/27/health/turning-points-charlie-jabaley-hip-hop-music-mogul-inspirational-athlete.

6. Burgis, *Wanting*, 137, 157–58.

7. Duhigg, *Power of Habit*, 51.

Chapter 11 You Can Master Your Own Motivation

1. Kaitlin Woolley and Ayelet Fishbach, "The Experience Matters More Than You Think: People Value Intrinsic Incentives More Inside Than Outside an Activity," *Journal of Personality and Social Psychology* 109, no. 6 (2015): 968–82, https://doi.org/10.1037/pspa0000035.

2. Duhigg, *Power of Habit*, 51.

3. Anders Ericsson and Robert Pool, *Peak: Secrets from the New Science of Expertise* (New York: Houghton Mifflin, 2016), 172.

4. Dean, *Making Habits*, 5–7.

5. Quoted in Brad Isaac, "Jerry Seinfeld's Productivity Secret," *LifeHacker*, July 24, 2007, http://lifehacker.com/281626/jerry-seinfelds-productivity-secret. See also Dean, *Making Habits*, 131.

6. James Linville and George Plimpton, "Fran Lebowitz, A Humorist at Work," *The Paris Review*, Summer 1993, https://www.theparisreview.org/miscellaneous/1931/a-humorist-at-work-fran-lebowitz.

7. Ayelet Fishbach, *Get It Done: Surprising Lessons from the Science of Motivation* (New York: Hachette, 2022), 58–61.

8. Fishbach, *Get It Done*, 61.

9. See Dan Sullivan with Benjamin Hardy, *The Gap and the Gain: The High Achievers' Guide to Happiness, Confidence, and Success* (New York: Hay House, 2021).

10. Fishbach, *Get It Done*, 106–7.

11. Chris McChesney, Sean Covey, and Jim Huling, *The 4 Disciplines of Execution: Achieving Your Wildly Important Goals* (New York: Free Press, 2012).

Chapter 12 The Journey Is Better with Friends

1. J. R. R. Tolkien, *The Letters of J. R. R. Tolkien*, ed. Humphrey Carpenter (Boston: Houghton Mifflin, 1981), 23–24.

2. Tolkien, *Letters*, 38.
3. Tolkien, *Letters*, 166.
4. Tolkien, *Letters*, 184.
5. Tolkien, *Letters*, 362.
6. John Swansburg, "The Self-Made Man," *Slate*, September 29, 2014, http://www.slate.com/articles/news_and_politics/history/2014/09/the_self_made_man_history_of_a_myth_from_ben_franklin_to_andrew_carnegie.html.
7. Proverbs 27:17 ESV.
8. Proverbs 22:24–25.
9. Cloud, *Power of the Other*, 78.
10. Staats, *Never Stop Learning*, 157.
11. Walton, "What Happened to Your Goals?"
12. Derek Sivers, "Keep Your Goals to Yourself," TED, July 2010, https://www.ted.com/talks/derek_sivers_keep_your_goals_to_yourself.
13. Duhigg, *Power of Habit*, 85.
14. Duhigg, *Power of Habit*, 88–89.
15. Enrico Moretti, *The New Geography of Jobs* (New York: Mariner, 2013), 141.
16. Joshua Wolf Shenk, "The Power of Two," *Atlantic*, July–August 2014, https://www.theatlantic.com/magazine/archive/2014/07/the-power-of-two/372289.
17. The Samson Society (SamsonSociety.com) is an international Christian accountability group for men, founded by Nate Larkin.

Step 5 Make It Happen

1. Quoted in Rick Beard, "The Napoleon of the American Republic," Opinionator, *New York Times*, October 31, 2011, https://opinionator.blogs.nytimes.com/2011/10/31/the-napoleon-of-the-american-republic.
2. Stephen Sears, "McClellan at Antietam," American Battlefield Trust, accessed February 15, 2023, https://www.battlefields.org/learn/articles/mcclellan-antietam. For the complete story, see Stephen Sears, *George B. McClellan: The Young Napoleon* (New York: Ticknor & Fields, 1998), 270–323.

Chapter 13 One Journey Is Many Steps

1. Robert Marchant, "Greenwich Man, 71, to Run up Empire State Building's 1,576 Stairs—despite Replaced Hip, Busted Knee," *Greenwich Time*, October 4, 2022, https://www.greenwichtime.com/news/article/Old-Greenwich-1-576-stairs-Empire-State-Building-17478237.php.
2. See "Eat a Live Frog Every Morning, and Nothing Worse Will Happen to You the Rest of the Day," Quote Investigator, April 3, 2013, http://quoteinvestigator.com/2013/04/03/eat-frog.
3. Francesca Gino and Bradley Staats, "Your Desire to Get Things Done Can Undermine Your Effectiveness," *Harvard Business Review*, March 22,

2016, https://hbr.org/2016/03/your-desire-to-get-things-done-can-undermine-your-effectiveness.

4. Chris Napolitano, "Having a Backup Plan Might Be the Very Reason You Failed," *Aeon*, June 16, 2016, https://aeon.co/ideas/having-a-backup-plan-might-be-the-very-reason-you-failed.

5. W. H. Murray, *The Scottish Himalayan Expedition* (London: J. M. Dent & Sons, 1951), 6–7.

6. Beard, "Napoleon of the American Republic."

Chapter 14 Visibility Is Essential

1. James H. Doolittle with Carroll V. Glines, *I Could Never Be So Lucky Again* (New York: Bantam, 1991), 130.

2. Doolittle, *Never Be So Lucky*, 132.

3. Doolittle, *Never Be So Lucky*, 150.

4. Cheryl J. Travers, "Using Goal Setting Theory to Promote Personal Development," in Locke and Latham, *New Developments*, 603–19.

5. Christopher Bergland, "The Neuroscience of Perseverance," *Psychology Today*, December 26, 2011, https://www.psychologytoday.com/blog/the-athletes-way/201112/the-neuroscience-perseverance.

6. Karnazes, *Road to Sparta*, 108–9.

Chapter 15 You Can Trigger Success

1. Heidi Grant, "Get Your Team to Do What It Says It's Going to Do," *Harvard Business Review*, May 2014, https://hbr.org/2014/05/get-your-team-to-do-what-it-says-its-going-to-do.

2. Thomas Llewelyn Webb and Paschal Sheeran, "How Do Implementation Intentions Promote Goal Attainment? A Test of Component Processes," *Journal of Experimental Social Psychology* 43, no. 2 (March 2007): 295–302, https://doi.org/10.1016/j.jesp.2006.02.001.

3. Grant, "Get Your Team to Do What It Says."

4. Peter M. Gollwitzer and Gabriele Oettingen, "Planning Promotes Goal Striving," in *Handbook of Self-Regulation*, 2nd ed., ed. Kathleen D. Vohs and Roy F. Baumeister (New York: Guilford, 2011), 165.

The LEAP Principle

1. Clarke, *Profiles of the Future*, 1–11.

2. Quoted in Steven J. Zaloga, *George S. Patton: Leadership-Strategy-Conflict* (Oxford: Osprey, 2010), 12.

3. Michael Keane, *Patton: Blood, Guts, and Prayer* (Washington, DC: Regnery, 2012), 156.

4. "Patton's Career a Brilliant One," *New York Times*, December 22, 1945, http://www.nytimes.com/learning/general/onthisday/bday/1111.html.

Thanks

Let me tell you how this happened: Megan Hyatt Miller is my oldest daughter and the chief executive of Full Focus. In the fall of 2013, she said, "Dad, you have a unique approach to goal setting. I think we should interview you about that for Platform University [my former membership website]. We could use it as a master class in January." I thought it was a good idea, so I agreed.

A few days later, Megan ran the idea by Stu McLaren, our partner in Platform University®. He loved the idea but suggested we turn it into a stand-alone online course. We all got excited about it, and a few weeks later, we were in Toronto shooting it. Thus was born 5 Days to Your Best Year Ever™.

Since that time, more than fifty thousand students from over one hundred countries have taken the course. Out of its success we created a live event that we host in January. I also hosted a series of quarterly face-to-face workshops for several years for our most dedicated students, which eventually morphed into a full-fledged coaching program. Plus, of course, this book—here in its second edition.

None of this would have happened if it had not been for the vision, creativity, encouragement, and hard work of Megan and Stu. Thank you both.

My wife, Gail, is a constant source of encouragement. She is never afraid to speak her mind and express her opinion. But she always does it in a way that is loving and kind, something that has become her trademark in dealing with everyone who knows her.

Joel Miller is our chief product officer at Full Focus. He helped me stitch together this manuscript using the raw materials of my course, blog posts, podcasts, and webinars, and my interactions with clients both online and off. He has truly become my creative partner and collaborator. I am grateful for his ability to analyze, synthesize, and organize my content into final form. I can't imagine embarking on any creative endeavor without him at my side.

Joel worked with Jessica Rogers and Leeanna Nelson to complete this second edition—I'm grateful for their contributions.

My literary agent, Bryan Norman of Alive Communications, has become an invaluable part of our team. He has been involved in every phase of this project from ideation to publication. He is my trusted advisor for everything related to my publishing pursuits. Not only is he crazy smart, he's exceedingly responsive and near flawless in his execution. His quick wit and light heart are an added bonus.

I remain grateful to my first editor at Baker, Chad Allen, for his vision, creative input, and patience in working with us on this project. He has been a literary midwife in helping me give birth to it.

I would also like to thank all my friends at Baker Books, especially Dwight Baker, Brian Vos, Mark Rice, and Kristin Adkinson. Their approach to publishing is uniquely author friendly. The first edition of *Your Best Year Ever* was our second project together. We've done several more since and have more to come. I am deeply grateful for our publishing partnership.

Dean Rainey of Rainey Media also had his fingerprints on this project. He helped shape the initial content of the course and partnered with us through every iteration of it. His coaching and belief in me have been invaluable.

I especially want to thank my 5 Days to Your Best Year Ever course alumni, including those who have shared their stories in this book:

Natalee Champlin (NataleeChamplin.com)
Ray Edwards (RayEdwards.com)
James "J. R." Reid (JamesReid.com)
H. Blake Edwards (www.HBlakeEdwards.com)
Sundi Jo Graham (SundiJo.com)
Scott Kedersha (ScottKedersha.com)

You have become more than my students; you are my teachers.

Finally, I would be remiss if I didn't mention my amazing team at Full Focus.

Index